Nuclear Notes

Volume 3, Issue 1

EDITOR
Sarah Weiner

CONTRIBUTING AUTHORS
John Edwards
Kristin Goodwin
Michael McBride
Blake Narendra
Idon Natanzon
Jonathan Papp
Raj Pattani
Marc Quint
Angela Weaver

A Report of the CSIS Project on Nuclear Issues

August 2013

50 YEARS | CHARTING OUR FUTURE

CSIS | CENTER FOR STRATEGIC & INTERNATIONAL STUDIES

ROWMAN & LITTLEFIELD
Lanham • Boulder • New York • Toronto • Plymouth, UK

About CSIS—50th Anniversary Year

For 50 years, the Center for Strategic and International Studies (CSIS) has developed solutions to the world's greatest policy challenges. As we celebrate this milestone, CSIS scholars are developing strategic insights and bipartisan policy solutions to help decisionmakers chart a course toward a better world.

CSIS is a nonprofit organization headquartered in Washington, D.C. The Center's 220 full-time staff and large network of affiliated scholars conduct research and analysis and develop policy initiatives that look into the future and anticipate change.

Founded at the height of the Cold War by David M. Abshire and Admiral Arleigh Burke, CSIS was dedicated to finding ways to sustain American prominence and prosperity as a force for good in the world. Since 1962, CSIS has become one of the world's preeminent international institutions focused on defense and security; regional stability; and transnational challenges ranging from energy and climate to global health and economic integration.

Former U.S. senator Sam Nunn has chaired the CSIS Board of Trustees since 1999. Former deputy secretary of defense John J. Hamre became the Center's president and chief executive officer in April 2000.

CSIS does not take specific policy positions; accordingly, all views expressed herein should be understood to be solely those of the author(s).

About the CSIS Project on Nuclear Issues

Many of the most pressing national and international security challenges are tied to nuclear weapons. The need to reduce the prevalence of nuclear weapons globally and prevent their use by states and non-state actors runs parallel with the need to maintain certain nuclear capabilities and the intellectual assets that support them. Both tracks present long-term challenges that, to be managed, will require sustained effort by talented and dedicated professionals. The Project on Nuclear Issues (PONI) seeks to help improve the effectiveness of U.S. nuclear strategy and policy through professional development and networking activities that target the next generation of leaders in the field.

PONI maintains an enterprise-wide membership base; hosts four major conferences and several smaller events each year; maintains an online blog; holds live debates on critical nuclear weapons issues; runs a six-month academic program for young experts; organizes bilateral exchanges involving young experts from the United States and abroad; and distributes regular news and event announcements to members. More information can be found at www.csis.org/isp/poni.

About Nuclear Notes

Nuclear Notes is a biannual publication of the CSIS Project on Nuclear Issues (PONI) featuring innovative thinking by rising experts. Its goal is to advance the public debate about nuclear weapons strategy and policy. We welcome submissions of 2,000-3,000 words on contemporary topics pertaining to nuclear weapons strategy or policy. Submissions can be sent to poni@csis.org for review by PONI staff and senior members.

Library of Congress Cataloging-in-Publication Data
CIP information available on request.

ISBN: 978-1-4422-2521-3 (pb); 978-1-4422-2522-0 (eBook)

Center for Strategic & International Studies
1800 K Street, NW, Washington, DC 20006
202-887-0200 | www.csis.org

Rowman & Littlefield
4501 Forbes Boulevard, Lanham, MD 20706
301-459-3366 | www.rowman.com

Contents

The Role of U.S. Nuclear Weapons in Assuring South Korea 1
John Edwards

Nuclear Command, Control, and Communication (NC3): Strengthening a Neglected, but Critical, Component of the U.S. Deterrent 9
Kristin Goodwin

Averting a Nuclear Arms Race in South Asia 23
Michael McBride

Restarting Arms Control after New START 30
Blake Narendra

Obstacles to a Middle East Nuclear-Weapon-Free Zone: Israel, Iran, and Beyond 38
Idon Natanzon

The Non-State Actor Threat to Pakistan's Nuclear Weapons 48
Jonathan Papp

Ballistic Missile Defense and the Iranian Threat: Key Issues 54
Raj Pattani

Defining the Costs of the U.S. Nuclear Weapons Complex: Reconstructing the 1251 Report 66
Marc Quint

Maintaining Nuclear Deterrence and Stability: Why the Status Quo of Nuclear Alert Rates Is Effective and Should Remain 73
Angela Weaver

The Role of U.S. Nuclear Weapons in Assuring South Korea

John Edwards[1]

The United States is moving forward with reducing the role of nuclear weapons in its national security strategy, which affects how allies and adversaries gauge U.S. commitment to the extended deterrence of South Korea. At the same time, many challengers in the Asian-Pacific region are increasing their reliance on nuclear weapons for their security. Russia continues to emphasize its nuclear arsenal to counterbalance an increasingly smaller conventional force. China is spending unprecedented amounts on its military, including improvements to its nuclear forces. And with a successful rocket launch and a third nuclear test, North Korea has inched even closer to achieving a nuclear weapons capability of its own. These countervailing trends stress the importance of understanding what parts of U.S. extended deterrence policy assure South Korea.

This article briefly examines the historic role of nuclear weapons in U.S. efforts to assure South Korea in order to maintain its nonproliferation posture and de-escalate crises. The piece accomplishes this goal by analyzing three periods during the past 40 years in which the value of U.S. extended deterrence came into question. Beginning with an explanation of extended deterrence and assurance, it reviews the turbulent 1970s period, the post–Cold War years (1991–2005), and then the new nuclear North Korean era (2006–2013). More specifically, the study focuses on the role of nuclear capabilities in diplomatic and military efforts in order to characterize their contribution to South Korean crisis de-escalation and nonproliferation.

Extended Deterrence and Assurance

Extended deterrence is the ability of a nation to deter an actual or threatened attack on an ally, while reassuring that ally of its commitment to the ally's defense. Assurance of the ally is an intrinsic part of an effective extended deterrence policy, in that the protected ally must be confident of the protector nation's will and capability to deter any attack.[2] One nuclear expert clarified it best when he described extended deterrence and assurance as

1. Air Force Lieutenant Colonel John Edwards is a former B-52 squadron commander who is completing a National Defense Fellowship at the Stimson Center in Washington, DC. His next assignment is on the Joint Chiefs of Staff, where he will serve as a future strategic concepts analyst.

2. Clark Murdock et al., *Exploring the Nuclear Posture Implications of Extended Deterrence and Assurance* (Washington, DC: CSIS, 2009), 1.

"two sides of the same coin."[3] If deterrence is about convincing an *adversary* not to attack, assurance is about convincing an *ally* that they will be defended in case of such an attack. This theory necessitates protector nations construct a nuclear posture around three additively fungible factors: general deterrence for the protector nation's homeland, plus extended deterrence (against an ally's adversary), plus assurance (to impart confidence to the ally).[4] While these factors are inextricably linked, efforts to assure allies are often considerably greater than what is needed to deter adversaries.[5]

The credible assurance of allies can take several forms but is primarily accomplished with diplomatic or military instruments of national power manifested by declaratory statements, formal agreements, alliances, dialogue, deployed or forward based forces, missile defenses, military cooperation, and combined exercises, to name a few. These various forms of assurance could be purely nonnuclear or could reference or actually include nuclear capabilities.[6] Hence, it is important to analyze the role of the nuclear component in the overall assurance effort. Since a major goal of assurance is to dissuade an ally from developing its own nuclear arsenal, this article examines cases beginning in the early 1970s when South Korea started such an initiative.

Assurance of South Korea in the 1970s

The 1970s presented several challenges to the U.S.–South Korean alliance. In the first part of the decade, the United States removed an infantry division from South Korea, which caused the Park Chung-hee government to question the U.S. commitment to South Korean security.[7] This sense of insecurity was the impetus for Seoul's initial venture into developing nuclear weapons, a feeling that was further exacerbated by the fall of South Vietnam in early 1975 when the United States did not aide its flailing ally. During these years, force reductions by the United States as a result of the Nixon Doctrine did little in terms of assuring South Korea; although some nuclear weapons did remain stationed throughout the region including tactical nuclear weapons on South Korean bases.[8] Yet, there was an incident shortly after the loss of South Vietnam that triggered a significant assurance effort.

The August 1976 murders of two U.S. Army officers by North Korean troops in the Korean Demilitarized Zone created a destabilizing incident that necessitated a strong

3. Franklin Miller, author interview, January 23, 2013.

4. Murdock et al., *Exploring the Nuclear Posture Implications of Extended Deterrence and Assurance*, 1.

5. Former British defense minister Denis Healey famously stated it took "only five per cent credibility of American retaliation to deter the Russians, but ninety-five per cent credibility to reassure the Europeans." Murdock et al., *Exploring the Nuclear Posture Implications of Extended Deterrence and Assurance*, 2–3.

6. Nuclear capabilities include nuclear-powered defense systems such as submarines and ships, which illicit similar responses as actual nuclear weapons.

7. Jeffrey Knopf, ed., *Security Assurances and Nuclear Nonproliferation* (Stanford, CA: Stanford University Press, 2012), 164.

8. In the 1970s nuclear-capable B-52 bombers were permanently based on the U.S. territory of Guam, U.S. ballistic missile submarines routinely patrolled the Western Pacific, and the U.S. maintained an arsenal of tactical nuclear weapons for use by artillery and aircraft based in South Korea. The Nixon Doctrine (or Guam Doctrine) displaced increasing defense responsibility from the United States onto its allies while re-emphasizing the protection afforded by the American nuclear umbrella.

response to deter further North Korean aggression and to assure the South.[9] The National Security Council recommended a strong military response, demonstrated by nuclear-capable airpower assets—B-52 heavy bombers, F-111 fighter-bombers, and naval tactical aircraft—which would underscore the possibility that the U.S. response to a future provocation might include nuclear weapons. The military operation, code named *Paul Bunyan*, was a success. While the United States demonstrated its nuclear prowess, its diplomatic efforts were focused on assuring President Park, who viewed the operation favorably. General Richard G. Stillwell, the United Nations commander, consulted with President Park throughout the planning stages of the military operation. This likely mollified his secreted desires to resume pursuing a nuclear weapons program. In the end, the demonstration by nuclear-capable aircraft was effective in persuading the North to issue a statement of "regret," which marked the first ever apologetic statement from Pyongyang since the Korean War had ended over 20 years earlier.

By decade's end, Carter administration proposals to reduce U.S. nuclear weapons deployed in South Korea were viewed by President Park as a further deterioration of the United States' commitment to South Korea.[10] Though the impact on military capability would be minimal, these actions caused significant psychological and political concern within the Park government.[11] In order to assure Seoul, the United States sent ballistic missile submarines to South Korean naval ports.[12] These moves assuaged Park, who likely viewed U.S. nuclear capabilities as an effective deterrent and adequate tool of assurance.

Post–Cold War Assurance (1991–2005)

With the end of the Cold War, the United States unilaterally began an effort to withdraw or eliminate several classes of tactical nuclear weapons from around the world, including artillery shells stored in South Korea.[13] This created an assurance dilemma between Washington and Seoul, who viewed the act as diminishing the U.S. security guarantee. Accordingly, in President George H. W. Bush's announcement of the removal of nuclear weapons from the Korean Peninsula, he purposefully omitted B-61 nuclear bombs.[14] Keeping these weapons in South Korea was important to President Bush, who wanted to ameliorate South Korean fears.[15] While it appeared the South Koreans desired to keep both nuclear capabilities for assurance, they likely perceived the B-61 bombs as having greater military utility,

9. A joint U.S.–South Korean Army team had entered the neutral area that separated the two Koreas to cut down a poplar tree that was blocking the view between a tower and observation post. While preparing to cut the tree, the combined team was approached by a large contingent of North Korean soldiers who assaulted the team, resulting in the deaths of two U.S. Army officers.

10. Knopf, *Security Assurances and Nuclear Nonproliferation*, 164–165.

11. Ibid., 165.

12. Hans Kristensen, "When the Boomers went to South Korea," Federation of American Scientists Blog, October 4, 2011, http://www.fas.org/blog/ssp/2011/10/ssbnrok.php.

13. Dick Cheney, *In My Time* (New York: Threshold Editions, 2011), 233.

14. Don Oberdorfer, "U.S. Decides to Withdraw A-Weapons from S. Korea; North Korea to Be Pressed to Halt Program," *Washington Post*, October 19, 1991.

15. Ibid.

both because they were able to reach any target in North Korea and because they had greater explosive power than the artillery rounds. In addition, U.S. Defense officials were highlighting new conventional weapons that were used to great effect in the recent Persian Gulf War. Washington presented these advanced technologies, to include newly proven antiballistic missile capabilities, to Seoul as potential substitutes for nuclear weapons. While Seoul would acquiesce to the U.S. move and accept enhanced conventional military capabilities, it "insisted that the country remain under the U.S. nuclear umbrella."[16] It is therefore reasonable to conclude that nuclear weapons, in different numbers and types, remained essential to the assurance of South Korea.

By 1998, the situation on the Korean Peninsula appeared to be improving as the result of the South Korean president Kim Dae-jung's "Sunshine Policy." Yet North Korea was increasingly frustrated with the Agreed Framework, which included a commitment by the United States to provide Pyongyang with energy assistance and two light-water nuclear reactors. However, due to suspicions that North Korea was moving ahead with its nuclear program, the United States delayed delivery of the reactors, a move Pyongyang viewed as breaking the framework. Without warning, at the end of August, North Korea launched a prototype ballistic missile that flew over Japan.

Both American diplomatic and military assurance efforts were insignificant compared to actions during previous crises. The U.S. approach mainly consisted of diplomacy, as demonstrated by Secretary of State Madeleine Albright who chastised North Korea for its action, urged it to stop missile development, and recommended it return to the Agreed Framework.[17] Most interestingly, the Clinton administration did not make any diplomatic pronouncements drawing attention to U.S. military forces and their role in extended deterrence. While the U.S. military's war plans were updated that year to "more clearly focus on offensive operations in North Korea," which was not an insignificant departure from its previously defensive focus, there were no visible military actions to assure Seoul.[18] This may have been because the South Koreans did not desire assurances or because American nuclear capabilities were already tied up in the Middle East and Europe in preparation for ensuing air strikes against Iraq and Serbia.[19] Furthermore, Washington likely tempered its assurance efforts because it would have been viewed as divergent from Seoul's Sunshine Policy, which promoted increased economic aid to North Korea in an attempt to improve relations. In the final analysis, U.S. assurance efforts were minimal, and were devoid of any reference to the nuclear component.

---

16. "The Withdrawal of U.S. Nuclear Weapons from South Korea," Nuclear Information Project, September 28, 2005, http://www.nukestrat.com/korea/withdrawal.htm.

17. "Text: U.S., Japan, ROK Joint Statement on North Korea Issues," U.S. Department of State, September 25, 1998, http://www.fas.org/news/dprk/1998/98092501_elt.html.

18. "OPLAN 5027 Major Theater War—West," GlobalSecurity.org, May 7, 2011, http://www.globalsecurity.org/military/ops/oplan-5027.htm.

19. In October 1998 a B-52 squadron was deployed to the United Kingdom for Serbian efforts and a second to the island of Diego Garcia to pressure Iraq to continue weapons inspections.

Assuring South Korea against a nuclear North Korea (2006–2013)

After years of deception and clandestine development, North Korea successfully conducted a nuclear test in October 2006, marking the beginning of a nascent nuclear capability. The reclusive regime would conduct subsequent tests in 2009 and 2013, each one affording Pyongyang more experience as it edged closer toward a nuclear weapon.

Beginning with the first test, the United States immediately launched an assurance effort centered on nuclear weapons in its diplomatic and military approaches. President George W. Bush publicly affirmed the United States would meet the "full range" of its deterrence and security commitments to South Korea.[20] Later, Secretary of State Condoleezza Rice made "strong statements of assurance regarding the U.S. commitment to extended deterrence" in order to further demonstrate Washington's unwavering nuclear umbrella.[21] By and far, U.S. diplomacy focused on wielding the United States' nuclear arsenal. On the military front, nuclear-capable B-52 and B-2 aircraft continued their forward deployments to the U.S. territory of Guam, which had begun in 2004.[22] Other nuclear-capable forces were also used through the deployment of additional fighter-bombers to South Korea and the continued patrols of U.S. ballistic missile submarines in the Pacific Ocean, as part of their normal alert posture.

Despite the political magnitude of Pyongyang's nuclear test, South Korea never requested U.S. nuclear weapons or reinitiated an indigenous program. This signified great restraint on Seoul's part, as North Korea's test was an unprecedented crossing of a political "red line." While U.S. efforts clearly assured South Korea, some of Seoul's defense officials "asked for the term extended deterrence to be included in the joint communiqué" that was later released.[23] In short, the United States' nuclear-centric assurance strategy and Seoul's highlighting of extended deterrence illustrate the importance of nuclear capabilities in assuring South Korea.

In 2009 Pyongyang would again shock the world with its second nuclear test, which experts described as more powerful than their first one three years earlier.[24] Yet, U.S. diplomatic efforts were devoid of the nuclear component of assurance, as evident by President Barack Obama's tempered statement condemning North Korea's "reckless action," which stopped short of referring to extended deterrence or the nuclear umbrella.[25]

---

20. Keith Payne et al., *US Extended Deterrence and Assurance for Allies in Northeast Asia* (Fairfax, VA: National Institute of Public Policy, 2010), 10.
21. Knopf, *Security Assurances and Nuclear Nonproliferation,* 173.
22. Nonnuclear B-1 bombers were deployed sparingly during short periods when nuclear-capable B-52 and B-2 bombers were assigned to combat operations in Iraq and Afghanistan.
23. Knopf, *Security Assurances and Nuclear Nonproliferation,* 173.
24. Jeffrey Park, "The North Korean nuclear test: What the seismic data says," *Bulletin of the Atomic Scientists*, May 26, 2009, http://thebulletin.org/web-edition/features/the-north-korean-nuclear-test-what-the-seismic-data-says.
25. Barack Obama, "Statement by the President," The White House, May 25, 2009, http://www.whitehouse.gov/the-press-office/statement-president-regarding-north-korea; and Barack Obama, "Remarks by the President

Militarily, there were no overt displays of force, though nuclear-capable bombers advanced F-22 conventional fighter-bombers, and nuclear missile submarines continued operations in the region.[26] Any exercises that may have occurred between the United States and South Korea were unannounced. In this case, the United States favored a reduced role for its nuclear capabilities that may have been acceptable to Seoul, who after much resistance, finally joined the Proliferation Security Initiative and made no further moves against Pyongyang.[27] As nuclear capabilities quietly operated in the background, the crisis abated with no further escalation between the two sides for the time being.

In early 2013 North Korea announced its third nuclear test, accomplished with a smaller, but more powerful device, thus signifying progress in its nuclear weapons program.[28] The nuclear test spurred additional United Nations' sanctions, which in turn served as North Korea's justification for its ensuing vitriolic statements, even more belligerent than those in recent years. For the first time, Pyongyang threatened to "launch a pre-emptive nuclear strike against the United States and South Korea."[29]

U.S. assurance efforts were swift and powerful. President Obama stated that the "highly provocative act" would "undermine regional stability" and constitute "a threat to U.S. national security."[30] More notably, he referenced the "extended deterrence offered by the U.S. nuclear umbrella" in a phone call to South Korea's president.[31] In response to Pyongyang's bellicose rhetoric, the United States publicly declared that it flew nuclear-capable B-52 and B-2 bombers over South Korea, deployed F-22 fighter-bombers to the South, contributed a nuclear attack submarine to an ongoing military exercise, and then moved additional ballistic missile defense ships to the area.[32] These powerful displays of the United States' most advanced and expensive military hardware illustrated its pledge to defend South Korea. Furthermore, the publicly declared over-flights by nuclear-capable bombers and operations by a nuclear attack submarine highlight the prominence of

---

on North Korea," The White House, May 25 2009, http://www.whitehouse.gov/the-press-office/remarks-president-north-korea.

26. Georganne Schultz, "Airmen, F-22s support Pacific presence mission," *Air Force Print News*, May 29, 2009, http://www.af.mil/news/story.asp?id=123151680.

27. "S. Korea to Join US-Led Anti-Proliferation Drill," *Korea Times*, May 26, 2009, http://www.koreatimes.co.kr/www/news/nation/2009/05/113_45671.html.

28. "North Korea nuclear test: no radiation detected," BBC, February 14, 2013, http://www.bbc.co.uk/news/world-asia-21455080.

29. Chelsea Carter, "What's in a threat? A look at North Korea's escalating rhetoric—and actions," CNN, March 8, 2013, http://www.cnn.com/2013/03/08/world/asia/north-korea-threats-timeline.

30. "Readout of President's Call with Republic of Korea President Lee Myung bak," The White House, February 12, 2013, http://www.whitehouse.gov/the-press-office/2013/02/12/readout-presidents-call-republic-korea-president-lee-myung-bak.

31. Barack Obama, "Statement by the President on North Korean announcement of nuclear test," The White House, February 12, 2013, http://www.whitehouse.gov/the-press-office/2013/02/12/statement-president-north-korean-announcement-nuclear-test.

32. Thom Shanker and Choe Sang-Hun, "U.S. Begins Stealth Bombing Runs over South Korea," *New York Times*, March 28, 2013, http://www.nytimes.com/2013/03/29/world/asia/us-begins-stealth-bombing-runs-over-south-korea.html?_r=0; Julian Barnes, "U.S. Ups Its Show of Force in Korea," *Wall Street Journal*, April 1, 2013; Barbara Starr, "U.S. moves warships, sea-based radar to watch North Korea," CNN, April 1, 2013, http://www.cnn.com/2013/04/01/world/asia/us-north-korea-radar/index.html.

nuclear weapons during this crisis. Following the B-52 flights, a South Korean Defense Ministry spokesperson stated the action "shows U.S. commitment to provide its nuclear umbrella," which further affirmed the dominant role played by U.S. nuclear weapons in assuring South Korea.[33] These strong U.S. assurance measures were welcomed by Seoul, who faced an increasing threat and internal calls to develop its own nuclear weapons program. In fact, a recent poll reported that 66 percent of South Koreans "support developing a nuclear weapons program" and that there has been a small decrease in South Korean confidence in the U.S. nuclear umbrella.[34] Obviously, it was critical for the United States to take these forceful diplomatic and military steps in order to deter North Korea, while also ensuring Seoul maintained its nonproliferation promise.

Conclusion

While U.S. assurance to South Korea has been tested throughout the decades, it is *clear* that both diplomatic and military means of assurance are underpinned by U.S. nuclear weapons in the form of extended deterrence. A National Institute for Public Policy report stated, "South Koreans see U.S. nuclear weapons as a deterrent to the North Korean attack," and affirmed that for South Koreans, a nuclear umbrella is more assuring than other forms of nonnuclear extended deterrence.[35] Yet it should be noted that while nuclear weapons are fundamentally key to extended deterrence, the same history has shown they must be part of a holistic approach. Official statements and forward deployments "virtually ensure U.S. involvement in any future Korean conflict . . . which lends credibility to the U.S. nuclear guarantee."[36] As South Korea enhances its conventional forces and develops missile defenses, it is unlikely "that they see improvement in nonnuclear capabilities as reducing their need for U.S. nuclear protection."[37] This is a critical point to keep in mind as the United States embarks on a course of reducing nuclear weapons' role in its national security strategy.

In the end, nuclear weapons play a *prominent* role in guaranteeing South Korea remains a nonnuclear weapon state and preventing crisis escalation. By invoking deterrence afforded by the nuclear umbrella and buttressing those statements with existing nuclear military capabilities in the region, the United States has shown that, on the whole, nuclear weapons assure South Korea in the face of a nuclear North Korea as well as further reductions in U.S. defense forces due to fiscal pressures. Yet, while the character of the nuclear component should not be overstated, neither can it be replaced by any other capabilities in the foreseeable future. As a result, the United States should *recognize* the increasing

33. Brad Lendon, "U.S. flies B-52s over South Korea," CNN, March 19, 2013, http://www.cnn.com/2013/03/19/world/asia/kore-b-52s.

34. K.J. Kwon, "Under threat, South Koreans mull nuclear weapons," CNN, March 18, 2013, http://www.cnn.com/2013/03/18/world/asia/south-korea-nuclear/index.html?iref=allsearch.

35. Kurt Guthe and Thomas Scheber, *Assuring South Korea and Japan as the Role and Number of U.S. Nuclear Weapons are Reduced* (Fairfax, VA: National Institute of Public Policy, 2011), 27, 32.

36. Ibid., 43.

37. Ibid., 32.

requirements stemming from extended deterrence and factor them into its future nuclear posture plans—both in terms of the number of warheads and, more importantly, in terms of the types of weapons needed. Otherwise, the United States could fall short of meeting its security obligations, resulting in allied proliferation of nuclear weapons and, more dangerously, a smaller crisis escalating to nuclear war.

Nuclear Command, Control, and Communication (NC3): Strengthening a Neglected, but Critical, Component of the U.S. Deterrent

Kristin Goodwin[1]

Introduction

For nearly 70 years and counting, the U.S. nuclear deterrent has been the cornerstone of the nation's defense strategy. Throughout this time, the true enabler of the nation's nuclear deterrent has not just been the weapons systems that are the focus of much public attention, but, rather, the infrastructure and people entrusted with nuclear command, control, and communication (NC3).[2] These highly skilled professionals have worked behind the scenes—often unseen and unheard—entrusted with, and ensuring, the ultimate guarantor of the nation's security. However, the fiscal challenges the nation now faces will likely result in significant changes and reductions in U.S. military capabilities. This "new reality" for the new century makes it particularly necessary to highlight the critical nature of NC3 in maintaining the credibility of the U.S. nuclear deterrent and to focus a spotlight on how to better support and resource this critical part of the nuclear enterprise.

Despite the absence of widespread public recognition, the personnel and technical systems of the U.S. NC3 are integral parts of the deterrent force and, consequently, U.S. national security. Even as the United States pursues a "world without nuclear weapons," it is unquestionable that as long as nuclear weapons continue to exist, the United States will need to maintain a robust and effective NC3 system that contributes to the deterrence of

1. Kristin Goodwin is a colonel in the U.S. Air Force. The views expressed in this academic research paper are those of the author and do not reflect the official policy or position of the U.S. government or the Department of Defense. In accordance with Air Force Instruction 51-303, it is not copyrighted, but is the property of the U.S. government.

2. There is not a clear timeline of when NC3 evolved from the nomenclature of NC2. NC2 represents the process and methods used to build/disseminate nuclear messages. NC3 represents the architecture and equipment used to send nuclear messages.

our adversaries and reassurance of our allies.[3] For this reason, the United States will continue to rely upon tried and true infrastructure and systems, as well as operators with years of experience, rigorous and comprehensive training, and the know-how to carry out the challenging mission they have been assigned.

The greater uncertainty in our profoundly changing world further underscores the necessity of NC3 that can be counted on to function across a range of scenarios that are more diverse than ever before. Emboldened adversaries with increased access to sensitive information and innovative technologies create new challenges and vulnerabilities. Most notably, cyber attacks on U.S. data systems are growing more sophisticated, numerous, intense, and targeted. New threats are also emerging in space, the operating environment of some of the military's most important technological assets. Our NC3 infrastructure and personnel cannot stagnate at a time when our nuclear enterprise must adapt to this new and quickly changing security environment.

Unfortunately, our aging, Cold War–era NC3 system may prove unequal to these emerging challenges. The time has come to modernize and evolve the current system into a more comprehensive and cohesive set of systems that will continue to be cross-cutting, redundant, survivable, and reliable, while providing the added benefits of a singular oversight mechanism. To be clear, this is not an argument in favor of reducing the number of backup components of the NC3 systems or of embarking on a "top to bottom" replacement of equipment. While full utilization of benefits offered by more efficient integration of modern capabilities and technologies should be pursued as much as fiscally possible, the first step is to simplify and refocus the complex nature of the nuclear enterprise. By necessity, the NC3 architecture requires diverse and redundant processes, designed separately, to prevent any common mode failures or singular threat vectors from potentially degrading its effectiveness. This argument supports centralized program management and greater control over the historically fragmented authority of the NC3 mission so that as the NC3 infrastructure is modernized and improved, so too is the management of the vital human assets within the nuclear enterprise.

To this end, U.S. NC3 should be carefully reexamined. Our nuclear infrastructure should be upgraded, our oversight mechanisms should be modified, and a four-pillar training approach should be established to preserve the human capital of the U.S. nuclear enterprise. The four-pillar approach should entail the following changes: a nuclear center of excellence should be established as an introductory and advanced-course training school for all current and incoming NC3 personnel; NC3 positions and functions across the various combatant commands (COCOMs) should be standardized; personnel tracking procedures should be established by each of the services and should be integrated for Joint Staff assignments; and a joint functional manager that provides uniformity and establishes joint nuclear coding across all of the services should be created. By implementing these

3. Barack Obama, "Remarks by President Barack Obama, Prague, Czech Republic," The White House, April 5, 2009, http://www.whitehouse.gov/the_press_office/Remarks-By-President-Barack-Obama-In-Prague-As-Delivered.

changes to NC3 infrastructure, oversight, and training, the Department of Defense (DOD) will be able to reverse the "cumulative loss of focus, expertise and excellence on nuclear matters in the United States" and will enable the long-term sustainability of one of the areas of expertise most critical to supporting U.S. national security.[4] As we, as a nation, adapt to and address the evolving security challenges of the twenty-first century, we must remember deterrence will only remain as reliable and robust as our nuclear infrastructure and the personnel we entrust to operate and maintain that infrastructure.

Historical Overview

Until the enactment of the Department of Defense Reorganization Act of 1958, nearly 15 years after the first deployment of atomic weapons, the United States lacked a systematic approach to the command and control (C2) of its military—and most notably its nuclear forces. Prior to this time, individual departments were responsible for designing and introducing their own C2 elements. This resulted in the ad hoc and decentralized creation of the nation's C2 systems, leading to inefficiencies and frequent incompatibilities between the equipment used by separate departments. Even after President Dwight Eisenhower signed the Act into law in 1958, interservice rivalry prevented true consolidation of the national command system.[5] One example of mismanagement was the Minimum Essential Emergency Communications Network that was designed to provide the president with the ability to communicate with strategic nuclear forces "during and after a nuclear attack."[6] Developed concurrently, but separately, by the Department of the Navy and the Department of the Air Force, the services' networks and infrastructure were entirely incompatible with each other. It was not until the 1970s, after the priority of the national command system was elevated and regional commanders were required to put the national system's requirements ahead of their own individual missions, that the systems were finally integrated.[7] Unfortunately, despite some progress, disconnected ways of thinking persist, with C2 staffs across the COCOMs focused more heavily on full spectrum operations in their own areas of responsibility, often to the detriment of the nuclear mission. Additionally, organizations whose primary focuses are nonnuclear have been assigned pieces of the nuclear mission.[8]

The Goldwater-Nichols Department of Defense Reorganization Act of 1986 marked one of the most substantial shifts in the history of U.S. military management. While the act restructured the U.S. chain of command, improved interoperability between the services in many arenas, and enhanced the centralization of command authority, lingering issues remained. With respect to nuclear command and control, the reforms of Goldwater-Nichols failed to

---

4. Department of Defense, *Nuclear Posture Review Report* (Washington, DC: Department of Defense, April 2010), 41, http://www.defense.gov/npr/docs/2010%20nuclear%20posture%20review%20report.pdf.

5. Bruce Blair, *Strategic Command and Control: Redefining the Nuclear Threat* (Washington, DC: Brookings Institute, 1985), 52.

6. Ibid., 56.

7. Department of Defense, "World-Wide Military Command and Control System (WWMCCS)," Directive 5100.30, December 2, 1971, http://biotech.law.lsu.edu/blaw/dodd/corres/pdf2/d510030p.pdf.

8. James R. Schlesinger et al., *Phase I: The Air Force's Nuclear Mission* (Arlington: Secretary of Defense Task Force on DoD Nuclear Weapons Management, 2008), 23–24.

establish a singular authority that would oversee the modernization and advancement of U.S. C2 capabilities. Although joint equipment development and procurement (along with total systems integration) were eventual accomplishments of Goldwater-Nichols, the act failed to standardize training or evaluation of the personnel involved in operating and maintaining the critical nuclear command and control infrastructure. It is important to note that, although the individual services and COCOMs follow established protocols for training and evaluating their personnel, they continue to design their C2 systems as their individual missions require, often ignoring developments in the other services or COCOMs. For these reasons, the C2 mission itself reflects the "patchwork" approaches of these past efforts and remains fragmented, lacking an overarching mechanism that could promote integration on matters where service equities overlap.

NC3 Systems

To provide a clear picture of the scope and complexity of the issue, it is necessary to review in greater detail the NC3 systems and infrastructure in place today.

The National Military Command System, "the priority component of the Global Command and Control System designed to support the Secretary of Defense and Joint Chiefs of Staff in the exercise of their responsibilities," is operated primarily from the National Military Command Center (NMCC), located within the Pentagon.[9] However, numerous additional ground-based facilities and airborne command posts serve the same function. These alternate sites include Site-R, located near Fort Ritchie, Maryland; U.S. Pacific Command (PACOM), in Oahu, Hawaii; U.S. Northern Command (NORTHCOM), in Colorado Springs, Colorado; and the U.S. Strategic Command (STRATCOM) Global Operations Center at Offutt Air Force Base, Nebraska.[10] The nuclear mission can also be directed from additional distributed command and control nodes at other military bases.

In the event that these fixed facilities come under attack or are otherwise rendered unable to function, several survivable alternative command and control platforms exist that can continue to direct nuclear operations. U.S. NORTHCOM has oversight of the Mobile Consolidated Command Center, a road-mobile back-up system. STRATCOM has oversight of two airborne command posts: the E4-B National Airborne Operations Center, designed to house the national command authority in the event of a crisis or emergency, and the E-6B Airborne Command Post, capable of relaying emergency action messages to all U.S. nuclear forces.[11]

Nevertheless, despite the myriad C2 platforms that exist, there are common factors tying them all together: infrastructure and people.

---

9. Department of Defense, *Joint Publication 1-02: Dictionary of Military and Associated Terms* (Washington, DC: Department of Defense, 2013), 193.

10. Department of Defense, *The Nuclear Matters Handbook*, expanded ed. (Washington, DC: Office of the Assistant Secretary of Defense for Nuclear, Chemical, and Biological Defense Programs, 2011), 50–59, http://www.acq.osd.mil/ncbdp/nm/nm_book_5_11/docs/NMHB2011.pdf.

11. Ibid.

Persisting Challenges

People have been the core of the U.S. nuclear mission since the days of the Manhattan Project and Colonel Paul Tibbets' 509th Composite Group in the 1940s. The nuclear mission and especially its people received top priority in funding and training throughout the Cold War. Although the nuclear mission has continued to be of national importance, both the NC3 infrastructure and human capital of the nuclear mission have experienced underfunding, undervaluation, and underdevelopment over the last two decades.[12]

SERVICE ISSUES

Once the U.S. military's premier mission, today the nuclear mission competes for scarce resources with an assortment of other global tasks.[13] Since the end of the Cold War, the criticality of the nuclear enterprise has received a general lack of recognition, and as such the services do not highly value the expertise gained by serving in NC3. Furthermore, as the nuclear enterprise loses its prominence within the services' budgets, the services have continued to merely assign personnel to a vacancy rather than put the "right person" in the right position with the necessary skillsets to meet mission requirements. The Air Force's new key nuclear billet process is producing solid results in placing critical skillsets in essential nuclear positions.

CONGRESS

Congressional appropriators have similarly fallen victim to persistently undervaluing NC3, largely based upon the lackluster interest demonstrated by the military in sustaining, adapting, and modernizing the system.[14] Political leadership and the general public tend to focus their interest on problems that are easier to define and approach, presuming that with the end of the Cold War, the United States does not need to continue to treat the nuclear enterprise with the same level of caution and consideration as in the past. This, coupled with the overwhelming emphasis on conventional military operations in the past 20 years, has perpetuated a culture of indifference whereby neither military nor political leadership prioritize the personnel within NC3, thus leading to the erosion of intellectual capital within the ranks of NC3 staff members.

HUMAN CAPITAL

The United States has lost almost a generation of nuclear deterrent practitioners and now lacks personnel with robust backgrounds in deterrence strategy and in the safety and security procedures and operations that were common in the past. This historical problem

12. James R. Schlesinger et al., *Phase II: Review of the DoD Nuclear Mission* (Arlington: Secretary of Defense Task Force on DoD Nuclear Weapons Management, 2008).

13. Schlesinger et al., *Phase I: The Air Force's Nuclear Mission*, 24.

14. Carnegie Panel on U.S. Security and Future Arms Control, *Challenges for U.S. National Security: Nuclear Strategy Issues of the 1980s: Strategic Vulnerabilities, Command, Control, Communications, and Intelligence, Theater Nuclear Forces: A Third Report* (Washington, DC: Carnegie Endowment for International Peace, 1982), 85–133.

must now, more than ever, be rectified to broaden and deepen the nuclear knowledge base within the armed services.[15] A clarion wake-up call to action in this regard was the unauthorized ferrying of nuclear cruise missiles from Minot Air Force Base (AFB), North Dakota, to Barksdale AFB, Louisiana, in 2007. That incident motivated the Air Force to set up a separate, nuclear-focused major command (albeit commanded by a three-star instead of a four-star billet as per the other major commands). There has been progress, but significant challenges remain for adapting NC3 capabilities to meet the needs of an ever-changing threat environment.

INSTITUTIONAL FOCUS

STRATCOM is but one example of the major commands challenged with broadening their focus from a singular nuclear mission to multiple missions. Initially created in 1992 to replace the now-defunct Strategic Air Command, STRATCOM's sole mission was to maintain U.S. nuclear deterrence.[16] Today, STRATCOM is tasked with three major mission areas: to "deter nuclear attack with a safe, secure, effective nuclear deterrent force; respond to the new challenges in space; [and] build cyberspace capability and capacity."[17] Moreover, STRATCOM oversees one sub-unified command and six components: U.S. Cyber Command; Joint Functional Component Command (JFCC) for Global Strike; JFCC-Space; JFCC–Integrated Missile Defense; JFCC–Intelligence, Surveillance, and Reconnaissance; the Center for Combating Weapons of Mass Destruction at Fort Belvoir; and the Joint Warfare Analysis Center in Dahlgren, Virginia.[18]

POLICY

While the 2010 *Nuclear Posture Review Report* briefly mentions U.S. NC3 systems, it simply notes that investments are being made to modernize older "legacy" NC3 systems and capabilities to "meet current and projected challenges" facing the United States and the nuclear enterprise, in particular.[19] Meanwhile, national security guidance continues to deemphasize the centrality of nuclear deterrence to U.S. national security. Certainly, adapting NC3 infrastructure and systems to function in the potential threat environments of the future is fundamental. Yet, the lack of discussion regarding the personnel required to man the systems is both problematic and emblematic of the low priority assigned to the NC3 mission. It is vital to ensure U.S. NC3 continues to receive the attention, resources, and support it needs and, indeed, demands.

---

15. Schlesinger et al., *Phase I: The Air Force's Nuclear Mission*, 22.
16. Strategic Air Command was both an Air Force major command and specified command, whereas Strategic Command relies on Air Force Global Strike Command to fulfill the major command responsibilities.
17. "United States Strategic Command: Mission," last modified April 2011, http://www.stratcom.mil/mission/.
18. "United States Strategic Command: Functional Components," http://www.stratcom.mil/functional_components/.
19. Department of Defense, *Nuclear Posture Review Report*, 26.

Recommendations

Many perceive the management of the nuclear enterprise as both complex and secretive. This, compounded with the enormous scope of nuclear issues, has led to a diminished understanding of the operation and importance of the nuclear enterprise. Nuclear matters must be, by their very nature, a "zero defect" regime—not a place where we find uncertainty. There should be clear oversight, service operability, and movement toward modernization that will keep the U.S. nuclear arsenal competitive, secure, and reliable against emerging threats. To bridge existing gaps the infrastructure needs greater integration through the development of NC3 equipment and standardization across the training of NC3 personnel.

There are concrete actions that can be taken to help combat the decline in NC3. Specifically, the focus on improving NC3 must be placed in three areas: infrastructure, which involves the design, acquisition, implementation, and/or leveraging of equipment and capabilities such as nuclear-certified hardware and software for connectivity; oversight, which concerns the people that have overall visibility into and responsibility for the NC3 enterprise; and training, which focuses on the people entrusted with the NC3 mission.

INFRASTRUCTURE

Classification issues preclude a detailed discussion of the U.S. NC3 infrastructure. However, it has historically been assembled as a patchwork, with NC3 systems at the various COCOMs put in place by a higher authority, but without real oversight or direction.[20] Although competition between the armed services can identify an array of feasible problem-solving approaches and can create new opportunities for cooperation or integration, it can just as easily lead to counterproductive rivalry and redundancy.[21]

Today we are operating and flying planes that were flown by our fathers and developed by our grandfathers. Equally, we are operating NC3 systems that were built and acquired starting in the 1950s, and procured in fits and starts in the decades since, with ad hoc solutions and Band-Aids developed as required to keep these systems operational.

The deputy secretary of defense has identified the need to integrate and reinvigorate the systems engineering capabilities across the NC3 network. The secretary's deputy chief information officer for command, control, communications, and computers and information infrastructure capabilities has charted a course in unifying technical authority that has not existed in the past, moving U.S. nuclear forces toward an organization that will increase service interoperability, oversight, and modernization. With a dedicated team of engineers orchestrating the current complex network of command and control, we can move to an efficient and modernized system that possesses the requisite capability necessary to meet

20. Blair, *Strategic Command and Control*, 53.

21. Ashton B. Carter, John D. Steinbruner, and Charles Z. Zraket, *Managing Nuclear Operations* (Washington, DC: Brookings Institution, 1987), 41.

the warfighting needs of combatant commanders. These measures are necessary and important as we move forward toward action and away from unhelpful rhetoric that distracts us from the importance of maintaining focus and monitoring progress.

OVERSIGHT

Once again, NC3 comes down to its core: people. The professionals entrusted with the operation of the U.S. nuclear deterrent and its command, control, and communication must be a top priority in both resourcing and training.

STRATCOM would be the seemingly logical choice to take on the mission of NC3 training. This option brings its own set of challenges about ownership and advocacy among the different COCOMs. As previously discussed, STRATCOM is already balancing time and resources for its six components and—although charged with maintaining the U.S. nuclear deterrent force—should not be singled out when every service and multiple COCOMs play a role in the completion of the NC3 mission. Instead, second only to the creation of a new, nuclear-only command, the Joint Staff should be charged with oversight of the NC3 training.

The Joint Staff is better able to provide guidance and assess the capabilities of the entire system by addressing NC3 with a systems-thinking approach and managing NC3 training. The U.S. Joint Staff's NC3 evaluation team (J36)[22] has the ability to identify potential weaknesses or shortcomings more quickly within NC3, allowing for greater efficiency while continuing to promote reliability, survivability, and credibility.[23] Having our nuclear enterprise's NC3 training in the Joint Staff is a natural complement to J36 evaluation responsibilities.[24] The evaluation team and the new training center can integrate the best practices in the field and incorporate lessons learned into a unified syllabus that serves as the bedrock for joint NC3 training.

TRAINING

Training of the professionals charged with carrying out the NC3 mission is critical. Improving training through a four-pillar approach ensures the future of the human capital within the nuclear enterprise is safeguarded. These include creating a nuclear center of excellence at the Joint Staff; standardizing NC3 positions and functions across the various COCOMs; establishing personnel tracking tools within each of the services

22. J36 oversees Command, Control, and Nuclear Operations on the Joint Staff and is responsible for advising the secretary of defense, chairman of the Joint Chiefs of Staff, and the Joint Staff director of operations regarding nuclear, space, and missile defense operations as well as all aspects of the National Military Command System.

23. Title 10 of the U.S. Code, Section 193 grants the secretary of defense the authority to, where he deems fit, assign the chairman of the Joint Chiefs of Staff to ensure that U.S. forces are trained, "capable of performing their support missions," and ready to "execute with respect to a . . . threat to national security."

24. Per the authority granted by Title 10 of the U.S. Code, Section 193, the secretary of defense should authorize the establishment of a Joint Staff nuclear training center in order to promote and support the people responsible for operating U.S. NC3 systems.

and integrated for Joint Staff assignments; and finally establishing a joint functional manager to provide uniformity and institute a joint nuclear coding across all of the services.

A Joint Staff Nuclear Center of Excellence

The United States needs a nuclear center of excellence in the Joint Staff to solve several NC3 personnel training challenges that the nuclear enterprise faces.

First, the United States must address the COCOM challenge. Currently, each COCOM tasked with the nuclear mission must divert the attention of some of its NC3 personnel to train incoming staff, decreasing the manpower available to perform other tasks. Furthermore, the burden of training may fall on instructors who have little or no previous experience training colleagues. Even the best instructors can suffer degrees of information loss, as one generation of NC3 staff can pass on only a portion of their own institutional knowledge before they are reassigned. This is particularly true for the unstructured, on-the-job training that prevails among today's NC3 personnel. Further, incoming command and control staff must undergo in-house training that caters to the operations and requirements specific to different COCOMS. This further distracts staff from the importance of the nuclear mission.

Following several severe incidents[25] involving nuclear weapons and nuclear-related material in 2006 and 2007, the Secretary of Defense Task Force on Nuclear Weapons Management reported, "Inspectors' lack of expertise has contributed to the diverse application of standards," further contributing to a culture that engenders a gradual decline in force readiness.[26] Although these failings were detected and addressed, they remain related to the infrastructure and physical components necessary to accomplish the nuclear mission. It is far more difficult to assess personnel and training standards. However, given the failures associated with the most visible aspects of the nuclear enterprise, one must wonder where else fissures have appeared but have yet to be addressed.

A Joint Staff training center would ensure trainers are highly qualified and promote greater operational readiness. Moreover, a center of excellence would also be responsible for ensuring that those tasked with evaluating others within NC3 are fully capable and given clear guidance so that similar issues do not resurface in the future.

Second, although the individual COCOMs and the services have made incremental improvements to their individual training and evaluation mechanisms, the nuclear enterprise as a whole lacks cohesive and coordinated top-down integration and uniformity or even a systematic mechanism for sharing and implementing best practices. There is no method to share information across the COCOMs to help improve the efficiency of

25. Barbara Starr, "Air Force investigates mistaken transport of nuclear warheads," CNN, September 6, 2007, http://www.cnn.com/2007/US/09/05/loose.nukes/index.html?_s=PM:US.

26. Schlesinger et al., *Phase I: The Air Force's Nuclear Mission*, 37.

Table 1 Notional NC3 Joint Qualification System

Position Examples	*Basic Course (NC3 100)*	*Single-Chair Course (NC3 20X)*	*All-Chairs Course (NC3 300)*	*Leadership Course (NC3 400)*
DDO	X	X	X	X
Strike adviser	X	X	Optional	X
EA controller	X	X	Optional	
SURVO/warning	X	X	Optional	
Comms	X	X		

Notes: Comms, communications; DDO, deputy director for operations; EA, emergency action; SURVO/warning, surveillance/warning.

management and operation. By creating a Joint Staff nuclear center of excellence to put top NC3 personnel, mid-level officers and those returning for further qualification, and incoming NC3 staff under the same roof, NC3 leadership will be able to develop an environment where the application of lessons learned to future training will pervade throughout the overall system. Primary nuclear education will supplement requisite in-house training at each COCOM and will simultaneously enable NC3-qualified personnel to transfer to postings at different COCOMs. This will also relieve pressure on the COCOMs by substantially reducing the amount of time and manpower needed to staff redundant training cycles of incoming NC3 staff. Lower requirements on the number of training hours and other resources devoted to training at the command level will give personnel time to focus on other critical aspects of their jobs and will make personnel management of the entire nuclear enterprise more efficient. Table 1 provides a notional NC3 joint qualification system.

By implementing standardized basic NC3 training taught at a centralized Joint Staff nuclear training center with a constant core of instructors, the nuclear enterprise will see tremendous gains in efficiency of trainer-hours spent per class. With a centralized school for nuclear training, class sizes could be kept small enough to provide clear and effective instruction and feedback, while limiting the redundancies of holding similar training at different sites. Preliminary evaluations and trainee feedback would further allow the Joint Staff to find the best trainers and determine which personnel should become full-time instructors for the NC3 staff for the duration of their assignments. Finally, the practice of sending individuals into critical NC3 positions without any prior experience or training will be eliminated, reducing the shell shock of being assigned to the nuclear mission. Under the stewardship of the Joint Staff, a nuclear training center would also be less likely to fall victim to the same increased mission complexity experienced by STRATCOM in the past decade. By implementing a building-block approach to NC3 training, the Joint Staff can begin to implement a best-practices approach to retain and cultivate talent within the nuclear enterprise across all the platforms and locations tasked with maintaining NC3 capabilities.

NC3 Positions: Standardization of Nuclear Positions/ Functions across the Enterprise

There are neither standard requirements for positions nor a nomenclature that is consistent between positions that perform the same functions across COCOMs in the 12 platforms and locations (illustrated in Table 2). This variation in position titles and ranks in the respective functions ensures a lack of consistency and can hinder coordination between nuclear command centers. Some individuals fulfill multiple positions during the same shift while others might have the same position title but be required to perform different functions. This is not acceptable. Generating requirements that favor innovation, taking a centralized approach while integrating the services' and COCOMs' respective efforts, will require an appropriate balance of support from all participants in the process. One major improvement would be to consolidate the personnel resources of the nuclear mission and establish a new joint nomenclature that is integrated and streamlined, thereby reinvigorating the capabilities of an atrophying industry while also facilitating the future improvement and adaptation of the system.

N Codes: Establishment of Nuclear Identifiers

The NC3 mission would be well-served by developing distinct career tracks that allow for professional development in the NC3 field, rather than sustaining the revolving door of NC3 operators that simply leave after receiving extensive training and expertise upon completing their assignments. Growing NC3 specialists and leaders requires service buy-in and senior leader support; however, it all starts with creating and supporting an NC3 specialty.

Creating an NC3 specialty will help to bring further depth and breadth into NC3 staffing assignments. It will allow for greater professional development as the best and brightest tasked with NC3 will eventually be able to rise to the level of trainers and evaluators. For example, the Air Force has tried to reverse the decay and the lack of expertise in nuclear leadership positions within the nuclear enterprise by establishing a Nuclear Professional Experience Code to facilitate the tracking of personnel with nuclear experience.[27] The other services should create a complementary system to better place individuals in needed NC3 positions to broaden and track their experience.[28] Granting NC3 staff greater recognition and development opportunities within their dedicated career fields also provides additional flexibility to develop as professionals, while simultaneously serving the needs of the NMCC and the COCOMs by enhancing the overall proficiency of NC3 personnel. Creating a nuclear coding system for military personnel will also help ensure that sufficient investment in nuclear-experienced staff is retained in the face of looming budget cuts and personnel reductions. The system could be reinforced by creating a manager responsible for the placement of nuclear-coded personnel.

27. The U.S. Navy has Additional Qualification Designators for the submariner career field to measure level of training and milestones, but it does not provide tracking of individuals in NC3 positions.

28. Defense Science Board Permanent Task Force on Nuclear Weapons Surety, *Independent Assessment of the Air Force Nuclear Enterprise* (Washington, DC: Office of the Under Secretary of Defense for Acquisition, Technology, and Logistics, 2011).

Table 2 Positions across Nuclear Command and Control Platforms

	Senior Adviser	*Team Lead and/or Conference Manager*	*Assistant and/or Conference Manager*	*Strike Adviser (SA)*	*Emergency Action Controller (messaging)*	*SOC (communications)*	*SURVO (warning)*	*NPES (N Plng / Exec Sys)*	*Staff Support / Surge*
Platform 1	*DDO (0-6/0-7)*	*DDO (0-6/0-7)*	*(O-5) (assistant)*	*SA (O-5/O-4)*	*EA ×2*	*2× Comm NCO: Generalist*	*SURVO (NORAD as backup)*	none	*"Ops Officer"*
Platform 2	*DDO (0-6/0-7)*	*DDO (0-6/0-7)*	*(O-5) (assistant)*	*SA (O-5/O-4)*	*EA ×2*	*2× Comm NCO: Generalist*	*SURVO (NORAD as backup)*	**Contract Support**	*"Ops Officer"*
Platform 3	*Team Chief (O-6)*	*Team Chief (O-6)*	none	*SA (O-5/O-4)*	*EA ×4*	*2× Comm NCO: Generalist*	none	*NPES×2*	**Staff Support**
Platform 4	**Commander**	*Team Chief (O-6)*	none	*SA (O-5/O-4)*	*EA ×2*	*6× Comm NCO: Specialist*	*SURVO (NORAD as backup)*	*NPES (×2-5 w/ surge)*	**Staff Support**
Platform 5	**DDO (0-6/0-7)**	*DDO (0-6/0-7)*	none	*SA (O-5/O-4)*	*EA ×1*	*5× Comm NCO: Specialist*	*NPES operator*	*NPES operator*	**Staff Support**
Platform 6–9	**Commander**	*Battle Watch Captain (O-6)*	none	*SA (O-5/O-4)*	*EA ×2*	*6× Comm NCO: Specialist*	*SURVO (NORAD as backup)*	*NPES (×2 w/ surge)*	**Staff Support**
Platform 10	**Commander**	**Branch Chief (O-5)**	**Branch Chief (O-5)**	**SA (O-5/O-4)**	*EA ×2 (×3/4 in surge)*	**EA**	none (NORAD as backup)	**NPES**	**Staff Support**
Platform 11	**Commander**	*Conference Manager (O-4/O-5)*	none	*SA (O-5/O-4)*	*EA ×3/4*	*2/3× Comm NCO: Specialist*	*NPES operator*	*NPES operator*	**Staff Support**
Platform 12	**Commander**	**SA/Branch Chief (O-5)**	**Conference Manager (O-4)**	**SA (O-5/O-4)**	*EA ×2*	*2× Comm NCO: Generalist*	*SURVO (NORAD as backup)*	**NPES**	**Staff Support**

Notes: Italic denotes day-to-day operations; bold denotes surge operations. There is *no* standard requirement for positions, nor are there descriptions for each position. Most platforms have both day-to-day *and* surge numbers that are different. These are the most recent configurations; they can change as the platform deems appropriate. Where titles match in different columns of same line, the position is filled by the same person. Staff support functions vary by platform. For example, there is a weather officer on three platforms and some add extra EA or strike expertise. Comms, communications; DDO, deputy director for operations; EA, emergency action; NCO, noncommissioned officer; NORAD, North American Aerospace Defense Command; NPES, Nuclear Planning and Execution System; SOC, secure operations console; SURVO, surveillance.

Manager: Nuclear Functional Oversight

To ensure adequate oversight, a tracking database should be set up to promote the resourceful distribution of NC3-qualified personnel across COCOMs. By better promoting the opportunities for career development within the nuclear enterprise and expanding career progression opportunities, COCOMs will be able to draw on a wider pool of willing candidates for NC3 staff positions. Furthermore, additional professional opportunities will revitalize the diminished status of the nuclear enterprise and attract the top operators in the services. An NC3 functional manager would facilitate a more strategic and thought-out staffing plan while providing uniformity to a disjointed cross-service process. Greater promotion of the relevance and importance of the nuclear mission by the top levels of the DOD will also help NC3 personnel continue to compete with other, more highly visible career fields and reduce the perception of NC3 as a "dead-end" field.

Introducing these four pillars into the personnel management of the nuclear enterprise will preserve the status of the mission into the future, allowing the United States to face an uncertain and complex security landscape with the knowledge that the stewards of its nuclear forces are the best and brightest and will always remain poised for peace.

Conclusion

The nuclear mission cannot fail. It remains the only mission area in which failure can result in truly catastrophic consequences and directly threaten our survival as a nation.

Though often overlooked in policy debates surrounding the modernization of U.S. nuclear forces, the NC3 systems and personnel that support those forces represent one of the most important areas for investment that Congress can make regarding the future security of the United States. Managing the NC3 system, though important, is a decidedly unglamorous pursuit. Even the services that depend most on the continuous and effective operation of NC3—the Navy and the Air Force—tend to focus funding elsewhere. In part influenced by the operational and/or tactical perspectives from the conventional warfighting realm, this has led to a culture less focused on the "must get it done right the first time" perspective required for nuclear operations. Additionally, over the last 20 or so years, the services have in varying degrees seen the nuclear enterprise as an area for cost-savings—"bill payers" to support conventional capabilities. Needless to say, this emphasizes cost-efficiency over reliability and effectiveness in all operating environments. This fails to achieve either goal optimally due to traditionally separate development cycles and inconsistent acquisitions and personnel management. Placing NC3 under a more structured hierarchy, as outlined above, will help eliminate waste and foster a greater sense of responsibility and accountability for a mission that has been referred to as the "organizational orphan."[29]

The United States faces an increasingly multipolar world where the proliferation of advanced technologies and weapon systems has enabled comparatively weaker nations and

29. Carnegie Panel on U.S. Security and Future Arms Control, *Challenges for U.S. National Security.*

even non-state actors to exert an inordinate amount of pressure on U.S. national interests and security. In response to the evolving strategic environment of the twenty-first century, the DOD must refocus support for and integration of U.S. NC3 capabilities to ensure they are robust, survivable, assured, adaptable, and agile across the full range of deterrent and employment scenarios. The overarching imperative, as stated in presidential directives across successive administrations, is to ensure that effective command of U.S. nuclear forces remains available to the president or the constitutionally designated successor at all times. Ensuring that NC3 personnel are provided with the best possible training and that the supporting NC3 systems and infrastructure are highly modernized and remain survivable is critical to accomplishing this task. By adopting several low-risk efficiencies, such as streamlining acquisitions processes for NC3 technologies and leveraging modern communications architectures; integrating the planning, design, and procurement of future NC3 systems; developing a nuclear personnel tracking and management system; and creating a Joint Staff training center of excellence, the DOD will be better able to provide the nuclear enterprise with the appropriate amount of support and attention owed to the nuclear mission and its people. With greater focus from senior leadership in both the military and government, the efficient management and operation of a system that has been plagued by problems stemming from the disjointed nature of its long history will finally be achievable. All of these features will be essential for the future of a system that cannot risk a single failure.

Averting a Nuclear Arms Race in South Asia

Michael McBride[1]

As nuclear proliferation has spread globally, potentially destabilizing new arms races have emerged between regional powers, most notably India and Pakistan. Since gaining their respective independence in 1947, Pakistan and India have fought four wars and countless skirmishes along their shared border. In 1974, when India tested its first nuclear weapon, Pakistan redoubled its efforts to gain military parity. It ultimately fulfilled Prime Minister Zulfikar Ali Bhutto's promise that the country would "eat grass or go hungry" to successfully develop nuclear weapons in 1998 when it conducted its own test. While an arms race has existed since 1947 between these two adversaries, the past several decades have witnessed an increasingly skewed and unconventional focus on nuclear weapons.

While neither Pakistan nor India pose an existential threat to the United States, a conflict between these two states that escalates to the use of nuclear weapons would significantly damage the international norm against their use, emboldening other states to use nuclear arms in future conflicts—including those that may involve the United States. It is at best uncertain if once either country employed nuclear weapons, the United States would be able or willing to intervene and deescalate the conflict. Given this reality and the inherent risks this poses to the international norm against the use of nuclear weapons, the United States must be aggressively involved in preventing the degradation of this norm. It is imperative that the United States aids in mitigating the risk of nuclear war between India and Pakistan through diplomatic and economic pressure to forge agreements regarding nuclear weapons doctrine; limit future production and research of new weapons and technology with the aim of eventual disarmament; and provide technology, economic aid, and technical expertise for the safeguard of nuclear weapons and establishment of deliberate decisionmaking systems to prevent accidental or hasty launches.

Both Pakistan and India have formidable nuclear weapons arsenals. It is estimated that the Pakistani nuclear arsenal currently consists of approximately 90 to 110 nuclear warheads. Pakistan possesses enough fissile material to produce up to 240 warheads; however,

1. Michael McBride, a former U.S. Army infantry officer, consults for the Department of Defense on security issues in South Asia.

it likely lacks enough delivery vehicles to take advantage of this stockpile.[2] Pakistan produces enough fissile material annually for approximately 10 to 21 warheads, depending on their size.[3] Currently, it is believed that India possesses 60 to 80 nuclear warheads, of which 50 are operationally deployed. Estimates of India's fissile material stockpile range from 1,500 to 3,300 kilograms (kg) of highly enriched uranium (HEU) and from 360 to 720 kg of plutonium.[4] However, like Pakistan, it is assessed that India does not have enough delivery vehicles for all its fissile materials.[5]

Pakistan has two primary delivery vehicles for its nuclear warheads: surface-to-surface missiles and aircraft. Pakistan has three nuclear-capable aircraft, the U.S. F-16 A/B, the French Mirage V, and the Chinese A-5 Fantan.[6] Pakistan's ballistic missile arsenal consists primarily of short- and medium-range missiles that serve both tactical and strategic deterrence functions. The Hatf short-range series of missiles has ranges of 70 to 750 kilometers (km), capable of carrying single warhead payloads ranging from 250 to 700 kg.[7] Of note, the successfully tested Hatf IX Nasr is a short-range, surface-to-surface, multi-tube ballistic missile with a range of 60 km. Given its range, it is likely that its primary purpose is to serve as a tactical delivery vehicle aimed at enemy troop formations.[8] Pakistan's arsenal of intermediate-range ballistic missiles can reach targets up to 3,500 km away,[9] thus capable of striking any potential target inside of India with a warhead up to 700 kg with a 35 kiloton (kt) yield.[10]

India's primary delivery vehicles are nuclear-capable aircraft and ballistic missiles; however New Delhi is actively working to develop the ability to deploy a submarine-launched ballistic missile (SLBM). India has five nuclear-capable aircraft—the Mirage 2000, MiG-27, MiG-29, Su-30, and Jaguar—and is actively expanding its fleet.[11] In January 2012 India announced plans to purchase 126 nuclear-capable Rafale fighter-bombers from France.[12] India's current ballistic missile arsenal consists of short- and intermediate-range missiles, but it is advancing its intercontinental ballistic missile (ICBM) development program. The Prithvi series of missiles are short-range, road-mobile ballistic missiles that are capable of being ground- or ship-launched and can carry a single warhead with up to a

2. International Panel on Fissile Materials, "Countries: Pakistan," February 3, 2013, http://fissilematerials.org/countries/pakistan.html.

3. Robert Norris and Hans Kristensen, "Nuclear Notebook: Pakistan's Nuclear Forces, 2011," *Bulletin of the Atomic Scientists* 67, no. 4 (2011): 93.

4. International Panel on Fissile Materials, "Countries: India," February 4, 2013, http://fissilematerials.org/countries/india.html.

5. Robert Norris and Hans Kristensen, "Nuclear Notebook: Indian Nuclear Forces, 2012," *Bulletin of the Atomic Scientists* 68, no. 4 (2012): 96.

6. Joseph Cirincione et al., *Deadly Arsenals: Nuclear, Biological, and Chemical Threats*, 2nd ed. (Washington, DC: Carnegie Endowment for International Peace, 2005), 239.

7. Missile Threat, "Missiles of the World," January 5, 2013, http://missilethreat.com/missiles-of-the-world/.

8. Norris and Kristensen, "Nuclear Notebook: Pakistan's Nuclear Forces, 2011," 96.

9. Missile Threat, "Hatf 5 Ghauri," November 13, 2012, http://missilethreat.com/missiles/haft-5-ghauri/?country=pakistan#pakistan.

10. Ibid.

11. Cirincione et al., *Deadly Arsenals*, 221.

12. Norris and Kristensen, "Nuclear Notebook: Indian Nuclear Forces, 2012," 97.

1,000 kg, 1 to 20 kt yield nuclear weapon.[13] The Agni-1 is a short-range, road- or rail-mobile ballistic missile with a range of 700 to 1,200 km capable of carrying a single warhead with up to a 2,000 kg, 20 or 45 kt yield nuclear weapon.[14] Notably, these missiles are short range, are able to carry a relatively small warhead, and possess a level of accuracy to suggest their primary use would be at the tactical level on the battlefield rather than strategically for deterrence. The Agni-2 is an intermediate, road- or rail-mobile ballistic missile capable of carrying a single warhead with up to a 1,000 kg, 150 or 200 kt nuclear weapon with a range of 2,000 to 3,500 km, making it capable of hitting any target inside of Pakistan. [15]

The Sagarika and Dhanush ballistic missiles are ship- or submarine-launched missiles. The Sagarika has a range of 700 km carrying a warhead between 500 and 800 kg[16]; the Dhanush has a range of 250 to 350 km carrying a single warhead between 500 and 1,000 kg.[17] As of this writing, the Indian government has declared that its SLBM-capable submarine *Arihant* will be inducted by the middle of 2013, a development that Pakistan has warned would be "destabilizing."[18] India is also in the process of developing several ICBMs, including the Surya-1/2 and Agni-5. Considering India's ability to reach all targets inside of Pakistan with intermediate-range ballistic missiles, it is likely that these new weapon systems are being produced to counter China, another geopolitical rival of India.[19]

The ballistic missile capabilities of India and Pakistan pose certain risks in the potential escalation of a conflict between the two countries from the conventional to the nuclear realm. The possession of significant short-range missiles increases the risk that tactical nuclear weapons might be introduced in a conflict, which could further risk escalation to nuclear war. This holds true especially for Pakistan because it cannot match the size of India's conventional forces. Compared to Pakistan, India has a larger population from which it can conscript soldiers and a stronger economy to support the purchase of more and higher quality conventional arms and advanced weapon systems. The reliance of both countries on missiles also raises the concern that a conventional ballistic missile might be mistaken for a nuclear-armed ballistic missile, potentially triggering the launch of a nuclear weapon in response to a conventional attack. Due to the geographic proximity of the two countries, the distance between launch sites and targets is quite short. Once a missile is launched, the other nation would have only minutes before impact, disallowing senior decisionmakers adequate time to absorb available intelligence and determine the magnitude and character of an appropriate response. This shortage of time could encourage leaders to overreact rather than face the consequences of a significant military disadvantage.

---

13. Missile Threat, "Prithvi SS-150/-250/-350," October 29, 2012, http://missilethreat.com/missiles/prithvi-ss-150-250-350/?country=india#india.
14. Missile Threat, "Agni-1," October 8, 2012, http://missilethreat.com/missiles/agni-1/?country=india#india.
15. Missile Threat, "Agni-2," October 8, 2012, http://missilethreat.com/missiles/agni-2/?country=india#india.
16. Missile Threat, "Sagarika," October 29, 2012, http://missilethreat.com/missiles/sagarika-k-15/.
17. Missile Threat, "Dhanush," October 8, 2012, http://missilethreat.com/missiles/dhanush/?country=india#india.
18. Norris and Kristensen, "Nuclear Notebook: Indian Nuclear Forces, 2012," 99.
19. Ibid.

India and Pakistan have not signed the Nuclear Nonproliferation Treaty (NPT), nor have they signed the Comprehensive Test Ban Treaty (CTBT). Pakistan is also actively opposed to joining the Fissile Material Cut-off Treaty (FMCT) noting that, if signed, it would place the country at a permanent nuclear disadvantage relative to India. India's strategic goal in maintaining a robust nuclear arsenal is to establish deterrence based on the ability to conduct retaliatory strikes against regional nuclear-capable rivals, namely China and Pakistan. This is confirmed by India through its "no-first-use" policy, declared in August 1999 and reaffirmed in official policy in January 2003.[20] In contrast, Pakistan has not publicly declared its nuclear weapons doctrine, which could inherently have a deterrent, albeit potentially destabilizing, effect due to its unpredictability. However, statements made by Major General Khalid Kidwai, the chief of Pakistan's Strategic Plans Division, provide some insight into circumstances which would lead to nuclear escalation by Pakistan. According to General Kidwai, "Nuclear weapons are aimed solely at India" and would be used if India occupies large parts of Pakistani territory, destroys a significant portion of the Pakistani armed forces, engages in an "economic strangling of Pakistan," pursues political destabilization in Islamabad, or otherwise encourages "large-scale internal subversion in Pakistan."[21]

Command and control over Pakistan's nuclear arsenal resides with the National Command Authority, comprised of 10 senior civilian and military officials with the prime minister serving as chairman. The National Command Authority consists of two bodies: the Employment Control Committee, which develops nuclear strategy and authorizes the use of weapons, and the Development Control Committee, which focuses on weapons development. Both committees are chaired by the prime minister.[22] During peacetime, weapons are stored unassembled with the warheads and delivery vehicles in separate locations,[23] which is significant because it would take several hours for Pakistan to prepare a nuclear weapon for employment. Pakistan's nuclear weapons are equipped with an indigenously produced version of U.S. permissive action links (PALs). Although designed to prevent accidental launch, their effectiveness is not known.

In India, the strikingly similar Nuclear Command Authority, a 10-member body made up of senior civilian and military officials with the prime minister serving as the chairman, provides command and control over India's nuclear arsenal. As in Pakistan, both civilian and military leaders have a role in the decisionmaking process to employ nuclear weapons, with civilian leaders possessing the final authority. The Nuclear Command Authority consists of two councils: the Political Council and the Executive Council. The Political Council, chaired by the prime minister, is the decisionmaking body, whereas the Executive Council, headed by the national security adviser, executes policy. Similar to

---

20. Suresh Dhanda, "Nuclear Programmes of India and Pakistan: A Comparative Assessment," *South Asian Survey* 17, no. 2 (2010): 264.

21. Paolo Cotta-Ramusino and Maurizio Martellini, "Nuclear Safety, Nuclear Stability, and Nuclear Strategy in Pakistan," *Pugwash Online*, January 14, 2002, http://www.pugwash.org/september11/pakistan-nuclear.htm.

22. Feroz Hassan Khan, *Eating Grass: The Making of the Pakistani Bomb* (Stanford, CA: Stanford University Press, 2012), 334.

23. Robert Norris and Hans Kristensen, "Nuclear Notebook: Pakistani Nuclear Forces, 2009," *Bulletin of the Atomic Scientists* 65, no. 5 (2009): 85.

Pakistan, India does not maintain its nuclear weapons on a heightened alert during peacetime, thereby limiting the risk of a hasty or accidental launch.

The United States should use its economic and diplomatic leverage to help diffuse the nuclear arms race and reduce the likelihood of a nuclear war between Pakistan and India. The outbreak of a nuclear war would invalidate international norms against nuclear use that have developed over the past several decades and pose a great security threat to the international community. The potential arms race could be diffused through the transfer of advanced technology and technical expertise that would prevent hasty launches and ensure no unitary actor has the ability to employ weapons, encouragement to change nuclear weapons doctrine, and the forging of new diplomatic agreements both between India and Pakistan and with the international community.

The United States possesses advanced technology and systems to ensure that the ability to launch nuclear weapons resides with multiple decisionmakers in consensus rather than a unitary actor. Currently India and Pakistan have a bureaucratic structure that ensures civil-military deliberations prior to the use of nuclear weapons, with a civilian leader making the final decision to use nuclear weapons. U.S. PAL technology ensures this mechanism is translated from the strategic decisionmaking level down to the tactical level, requiring multiple individuals to enter codes to activate nuclear warheads. PALs also introduce barriers to the use of nuclear weapons, thereby increasing the likelihood that the civil-military bureaucratic process would be respected. This is of particular concern with regards to Pakistan, where the military has seized political power several times in the past.[24] Transfer of PALs and technical expertise to both India and Pakistan would greatly reduce the chances of hasty nuclear escalation. Because PALs would apply only to preexisting weapons, do not make weapons more effective or lethal, and do not encourage or aid in the manufacture of new weapons, their transfer would not violate U.S. obligations under the NPT.

Pakistan's refusal to match India's "no-first-use" policy as a part of its nuclear doctrine fuels instability and raises the prospects of nuclear escalation. As part of a short-term strategy, the United States should apply significant pressure on Pakistan to adopt a "no-first-use" policy as a part of its doctrine. The United States should also press for an agreement to halt current production of all tactical nuclear weapons as a step toward the long-term goal of complete disarmament. This would increase stability and strengthen the international norm of utilizing nuclear weapons as a strategic deterrent and not a tactical tool in wartime. The United States is planning to provide over $2 billion in foreign assistance to Pakistan[25] and $98 million to India[26] in fiscal year (FY) 2013, money these governments use to provide basic goods and services to their populations and fund their militaries. Withholding or increasing this aid can be used to gain leverage in negotiations.

---

24. Owen Bennett Jones, *Pakistan Eye of the Storm* (New Haven, CT: Yale University Press, 2009), 284.
25. "Pakistan," ForeignAssistance.gov, March 27, 2013, http://foreignassistance.gov/OU.aspx?OUID=169&FY=2013&AgencyID=0.
26. Ibid.

As part of a long-term strategy, the United States should seek to influence strategic thinking regarding nuclear weapons among senior Pakistani and Indian officials. The United States has a strong tradition of incorporating international military officers in its professional development programs; foreign officers sometimes attend the Command and General Staff College and receive fellowships to study at the National Defense University. The United States should develop and offer education on strategic nuclear planning that focuses on strategic deterrence rather than tactical employment for senior officers of both countries. Influencing the thinking of senior-ranking military officers can have long-lasting impacts on the direction of technology development and the decisionmaking process surrounding the use of nuclear weapons.

Given its enduring conventional military inferiority to India, Pakistan's opposition to the FMCT is understandable: Pakistan relies on unconventional capabilities to provide for its national defense. As the treaty is currently constituted, it would extend this military disadvantage from the conventional to the nuclear domain, crippling Pakistan's ability to defend itself from Islamabad's perspective. Recognizing that India and Pakistan are already established nuclear powers, the United States must focus on arms limitation rather than disarmament. Rather than seeking to halt the production of all fissile material, the United States should work with both Pakistan and India to define and agree to an upper limit on the amount of fissile material to be produced and stockpiled, enabling each country to maintain an arsenal that would satisfy each country's desire for a strategic nuclear deterrent. This would promote regional stability, dissuade the use of tactical nuclear weapons, and serve as an important step toward the ultimate goal of disarmament. Movement on the FMCT might also create diplomatic momentum and lead to fruitful dialogue on the NPT and the CTBT. Failure to alter current policy will only result in the continuation of a nuclear arms race between two countries that lie outside international treaties and agreements. Negotiations with India over limiting stockpiles and the production of fissile material must also consider China, which India sees as a major regional competitor and a key driver in determining the composition and size of New Delhi's nuclear arsenal.

Using economic incentives, the United States should encourage Pakistan and India to establish a hotline between their respective prime ministers to facilitate immediate communications in times of crisis. Previous hotlines established between the home secretaries of the two countries to further collaboration on counterterrorism issues have been successful in forging trust and fostering improved diplomatic relations. Such a hotline could help to thaw tension between the two countries and help prevent nuclear escalation. Given the short time between the launching of a missile and its arrival at its target, an immediate method of communication between the highest levels of government is essential in preventing inadvertent nuclear escalation.

A major driving factor for both Pakistan and India to develop nuclear weapons was to gain international prestige and standing. While U.S. policy does not recognize either Pakistan or India as a nuclear power, it is perhaps time to reconsider this stance. Neither Pakistan nor India is likely to give up its nuclear weapons programs for any economic incentive or security agreement. The continued nuclear buildup—while neither country abides by the NPT, CTBT, or oversight by the International Atomic Energy Agency (IAEA)—is hazardous to the stability of the region and poses a risk to international security. The United States should offer to support recognition of either state as a nuclear power if it becomes a signatory to the NPT, the CTBT, and the aforementioned amended FMCT. U.S. recognition of Pakistan and India as nuclear powers would give the prestige they seek while also obliging them to enter into negotiations in good faith on disarmament. Both countries are also struggling to provide energy to the burgeoning demands of their populations. As an added incentive for ratifying and adhering to these international treaties, the United States should offer assistance in expanding civilian nuclear power capabilities. Continued denial of these countries' status as nuclear states is not only contrary to reality, but it also encourages relationships with countries such as North Korea or Iran to provide a counterbalance to the already established community of nuclear powers. While such action may encourage other countries to pursue nuclear weapons as a means to gain international stature, the continued existence of de facto nuclear powers that exist outside of established international agreements poses a far greater risk to international security and stability.

In the contemporary geopolitical landscape, the greatest threat of a nuclear exchange between two countries resides in South Asia. Pakistan and India both possess significant nuclear arsenals consisting of short- and intermediate-range ballistic missiles as well as nuclear-capable aircraft. Given the prevalence of short-range ballistic missiles capable of delivering nuclear warheads, it is clear that their use remains a viable policy option for both countries. The introduction of nuclear weapons into a hostile conflict has the potential to shatter the nuclear taboo of non-usage as well as result in catastrophic death and destruction to civilian populations and infrastructure. It would also deal a significant blow to the nuclear nonproliferation regime by emboldening other regimes to seek nuclear weapons. The United States is in a unique position to influence both countries through diplomatic pressure and military aid to reduce the risk of nuclear use in a crisis or conflict involving India and Pakistan. Failure to do so risks destabilizing the region and bringing an end to norms against nuclear use—both consequences that would threaten U.S. national security.

Restarting Arms Control after New START

Blake Narendra[1]

Introduction

With the 67th senator announcing a "yea" vote to the U.S. Senate clerk, Obama administration officials gathered in the Senate Gallery and dispersed throughout the federal city, breathing a collective sigh of relief. On the final day of a lame duck session of the 111th Congress in 2010, the New Strategic Arms Reduction Treaty (New START), a bilateral accord with the Russian Federation, was ratified after months of intense scrutiny. If unremarkable in the limited scope of its reductions, the treaty's entry into force ensured a continuation of bilateral cooperation spanning back decades. However, part of what distinguished New START from its antecedent treaties was that it broke with the historical norm of relative internal U.S. consensus on bilateral arms control with Russia.

New START is not likely to be the only aberration in this past trend of bipartisan and bicameral support for bilateral arms limitation and reduction treaties. Rather, the Obama administration should anticipate that the ideological and political objections that emerged during the Senate advice and consent process for New START has created a new normal—should President Barack Obama sign another treaty with President Vladimir Putin of Russia, he must contend with a U.S. Senate bitterly divided on the question of ratification.

However, to advance President Obama's goal of a world free of nuclear weapons, his administration must first contend with its substantive differences with Russia. The principal difference in the official positions of the United States and Russia hinges on whether to include nonstrategic nuclear weapons (NSNW) in a post-strategic, follow-on treaty to New START. Only a comprehensive approach that treats NSNW reductions in the context of a larger dialogue on strategic stability will present the United States an opportunity to conclude a treaty. As any hypothetical decisions on these issues strike at the heart of collective security, U.S.-Russian negotiations must also meet the approval of the consent-driven North Atlantic Treaty Organization (NATO). Finally, the task of creating the space for an agreement is equaled only by the challenge of reconstructing a bipartisan coalition of 67 senators needed for ratification.

1. Blake Narendra is a recent graduate of the Fletcher School of Law and Diplomacy at Tufts University.

Shape of a Bilateral Agreement

The United States and Russia must weigh the comparative advantages and disadvantages of concluding a nonbinding agreement versus a binding treaty. President Obama reiterated his preference for a treaty in his June 2013 speech in Berlin, Germany. However, the president's advisers hinted that if a treaty reaches an impasse during U.S. Senate advice and consent, then an executive agreement may be used.[2] The first option is to pursue a nonbinding bilateral agreement that only governs NSNW reductions. This proposal is slightly different from the Presidential Nuclear Initiatives (PNIs) because President George Bush's 1991 unilateral declaration was not contingent on Premier Mikhail Gorbachev taking reciprocal action.[3] A major advantage to this approach is that it would allow the United States to bypass a contentious Senate debate. However, even agreements that do not require Senate endorsement are not completely divorced from congressional processes. For instance, Congress could prevent the president from implementing an agreement by withholding the funds needed to dismantle retired nuclear weapons. The House version of the fiscal year (FY) 2013 National Defense Authorization Act would have prevented the president from making unilateral nuclear reductions in conjunction with his forthcoming Nuclear Posture Review implementation study. While this language was never enacted into law, it is testament to the attempts Congress may be willing to make to reign in the president's arms control agenda.[4] Nonetheless, the almost immediate entry into force of an executive agreement is a unique advantage over a partisan and protracted debate in the U.S. Senate on treaty ratification.

One of the chief shortcomings of the PNIs was the fact that presidential directives do not carry the force of law, so they lack the permanence of a treaty. An appealing feature of New START is its strict Article XIV(3) provision that permits a party's withdrawal only if "extraordinary events . . . jeopardize its supreme interests."[5] No such threshold exists for an executive level agreement, raising the possibility that a future U.S. or Russian president could determine that the agreement is no longer compatible with the country's national interest. President Dmitry Medvedev's threat to withdraw from New START in 2011 proves that treaties are also vulnerable to evolving circumstances; however, in the 50 years since the Limited Test Ban Treaty of 1963, only the Anti-Ballistic Missile Treaty has fallen victim to a state exercising the "supreme interests" clause to terminate a bilateral treaty.

---

2. Adam Entous and Julian E. Barnes, "U.S. to Propose New Phase in Nuclear-Arms Cuts," *Wall Street Journal*, June 19, 2013, http://http://online.wsj.com/article/SB10001424127887324520904578554010643116452.html.

3. President Bush reportedly outlined the framework of the U.S. declaration the evening before a prime-time speech; Gorbachev withheld committing to reciprocal measures but strongly signaled that he was amendable to responding "favorably." See Susan J. Koch, *The Presidential Nuclear Initiatives of 1991–1992* (Washington, DC: National Defense University Press, 2012), 2–20.

4. Kingston Reif and Laicie Olson, "Analysis of the Conference Version of the FY 2013 National Defense Authorization Act (NDAA)," *Nukes of Hazard* (blog), December 20, 2012, http://www.nukesofhazardblog.com/story/2012/12/18/13338/593.

5. Ibid.

As both states configure their nuclear posture to respond to the breakout of a possible crisis, a nonbinding pledge does provide assurance that withdrawn NSNW could not be reintroduced in the future. Adding to the uncertainty of a pledge, evaluating compliance with agreed NSNW reductions is entirely based on each state's self-declarations—Russia's historical reticence to detail its progress on specific PNI commitments and its reliance on new weapons manufacturing over life-extension programs underlies the rationale behind a strong verification regime.

The most fundamental disadvantage to concluding an agreement covering only NSNW is that it fails to account for Russia's complex security interests. The "irreversible" removal of 150 U.S. B-61s and dismantlement of the 500 in reserve is not sufficient to entice Russia to loosen its grip on its own NSNW. Russian military leaders would balk at a proposal that requires sacrifices without corresponding changes to the U.S. strategic posture. While Russia certainly perceives NATO enlargement and Europe's nuclear mission as a security threat, it also seeks a comprehensive agreement that addresses other strategic deficiencies relative to the United States. Most of all, Russia's military planners assess that the United States has the capacity to launch a devastating counterforce nuclear first strike. They base this assertion on the fact that the United States maintains a sizable "hedge" of strategic warheads that could be uploaded onto deployed intercontinental ballistic missiles (ICBMs) and submarine-launched ballistic missiles (SLBMs). While the Obama administration has "de-MIRVed" nearly all of its ICBMs so each missile only contains one warhead, Russia still views U.S. nondeployed warheads as a potential risk.[6] Ultimately, President Putin will not negotiate away his key NSNW bargaining chip unless the United States takes action that reduces the threat to the survivability of Russia's nuclear forces in a crisis.

The alternative approach, and one publicly favored by both U.S. and Russian leaders, is to negotiate bilateral reductions through a binding treaty. The two parties would agree to a central cap on total warheads. As of summer 2012 both sides possessed an estimated active arsenal of 4,500 warheads. However, the compositions of these stockpiles were very different. Table 1 shows that the United States maintains a substantial strategic hedge, whereas Russia possesses a far superior NSNW stockpile. A treaty should also encompass conventional precision weapons, such as those developed under the U.S. Prompt Global Strike Program. The program is already vulnerable to sequester cuts and the billion-dollar price tag per unit will limit its eventual deployment.[7]

The United States should attempt to negotiate a bilateral central cap of 3,000 active warheads with Russia.[8] A treaty that institutes a central cap of 3,000 active warheads builds flexibility into a reduction regime while correcting for the existing asymmetry between strategic and nonstrategic weapons. Given that Russia is already beneath the New START limits on deployed strategic warheads, reductions to meet a central cap would be

6. Hans M. Kristensen, *Trimming Nuclear Excess: Options for Further Reductions of U.S. and Russian Nuclear Forces* (Washington, DC: Federation of American Scientists, 2012), 16.
7. Linton Brooks, telephone interview by author, Somerville, MA, December 15, 2012.
8. Active warheads include all those that are not retired or slotted for dismantlement.

Table 1 Warhead Estimates, 2012

	United States	*Russia*
Strategic warheads	4,154 (1,722)*	2,440 (1,499)
Nonstrategic warheads	500	~2,000
Active stockpile	4,654	~4,500
Retired/awaiting dismantlement	~3,000	~4,000
Total inventory	~7,700	~8,500
Proposed active limit	**3,000**	**3,000**

*Parenthetical number denotes actively deployed strategic nuclear warheads.
Source: Hans M. Kristensen, *Trimming Nuclear Excess: Options for Further Reductions of U.S. and Russian Nuclear Forces* (Washington, DC: Federation of American Scientists, 2012), 13.

extracted from its NSNW warheads, thereby fulfilling a major objective of U.S. and NATO negotiators. Similarly, Russia's interests would be served because it requires cuts to the U.S. nondeployed strategic warheads even after a hypothetical wholesale retirement of its NSNWs.

The recently released Nuclear Posture Review Implementation Study should serve as the opening salvo into negotiations with Russia.[9] The United States should begin by negotiating a memorandum of understanding with Russia that details the precise size and locations of the two parties' nuclear stockpiles, broken down by strategic and nonstrategic warheads. This would involve detailing the number of Russia NSNW that are located in three different types of facilities. The category that generates the greatest fear among NATO members is the nondeployed active NSNW that are located in Russian naval and air force bases under the jurisdiction of the 12th Directorate.[10] The equivalent for NATO would be to share information on the location and number of the estimated 150 B-61 U.S. bombs deployed at six bases in five Europeans countries. The second reciprocal exchange of information would pertain to nondeployed, nonactive "reserve" NSNW in central storage in Russia and at facilities in the United States. Lastly, the initial data exchange should detail the number of NSNW slotted for dismantlement at each side's respective disassembly facilities. One major risk of the mutual disclosure is that it could expose the fact that Russia has failed to fully comply with its PNIs. Such a revelation could create the perception within the United States that Russia's inability to abide by past agreements makes it an unreliable negotiating partner in the future. However, while it is clear Russia has exhibited imperfect compliance in the past, it has succeeded in making a dramatic tenfold cut to its NSNW stockpile from an estimated 20,000 to 2,000.[11]

9. "Fact Sheet: Nuclear Weapons Employment Strategy of the United States," The White House: Office of the Press Secretary, http://www.whitehouse.gov/the-press-office/2013/06/19/fact-sheet-nuclear-weapons-employment-strategy-united-states.html.

10. Steven Pifer, interview by author, Washington, DC, February 22, 2013.

11. Hans M. Kristensen, "FAS Report on Status and Trends of U.S. and Russian Non-Strategic Nuclear Weapons" (briefing presented before United States Senate, May 3, 2012).

Framework for a Verification Regime

A key challenge is that all bilateral nuclear pacts between the United States and Russia have encompassed only strategic deployed weapons. A follow-on treaty could inherit the same counting rules that pertained to strategic aircraft in New START. Just as individual warheads associated with strategic bombers were not counted, this new treaty could similarly rely on national technical means to count nonstrategic aircraft.[12] A New START follow-on framework would retain the same structure for verification of strategic weapons and systems while also permitting inspections of facilities housing active nondeployed and reserve NSNW in Russia, Europe, and the United States.

The current numbers and locations of all types of treaty-covered weapons should be disseminated through the Bilateral Consultative Commission for strategic warheads and delivery vehicles and the NATO-Russia Council for nonstrategic weapons and paired systems. The Intermediate-Range Nuclear Forces (INF) Treaty serves as a useful precedent for constructing a verification regime. The INF Treaty mandated the destruction of banned delivery vehicles and their associated infrastructure and installed a multilayered inspections regime. The INF Treaty allowed for "elimination inspections," which permitted state monitors to verify that a missile and its component parts were destroyed.[13] Similar access to dismantlement facilities should be granted to U.S. and Russian inspectors in a treaty capping nuclear warheads.

While political and legal sensitivities help explain U.S. and Russian reluctance to negotiate a dismantlement treaty, the two sides can draw inspiration from past agreements. For instance, trilateral declaration signed between the United States, Ukraine, and Russia in 1994 allowed for Ukrainian officials to observe the destruction of withdrawn nuclear warheads at one of Russia's disassembly facilities. The Trilateral Initiative was another attempt to develop a verification regime that gave each party near perfect confidence while mitigating the risk of exposing classified information. At disassembly facilities, U.S. and Russian inspectors would have employed gamma ray spectroscopy to "interrogate" a suspected warhead and match its characteristics to the signature of a known warhead type without actively observing its dismantlement.[14]

---

12. Hans M. Kristensen, "The Challenge of Categories: Possible Paths of Solving a Problem of a Lack of a Common Definition of Non-Strategic Nuclear Weapons," working paper prepared for "The Warsaw Workshop: Prospects for Information Sharing and Confidence Building on Non-Strategic Nuclear Weapons in Europe," Warsaw, Poland, February 7–8, 2013.

13. "Treaty between the United States of America and the Union of Soviet Socialist Republics on the Elimination of their Intermediate-Range And Shorter-Range Missiles (INF Treaty)," Bureau of Arms Control, Verification and Compliance: U.S. Department of State, http://www.state.gov/t/avc/trty/102360.htm.

14. Thomas Shea, "The Trilateral Initiative: A Model for the Future?" *Arms Control Today* (May 2008), http://www.armscontrol.org/act/2008_05/PersboShea.asp%2523Sidebar1.

The Politics of Arms Control

Even skillful diplomacy with Russia does not guarantee entry into force of a treaty. New START became an anomaly in a four-decade record of relative bipartisan consensus on U.S.-Russian arms control efforts. Seventy-one U.S. senators voted for ratification, with the entire Democratic caucus and 13 Republicans among its supporters. Save for some skillful maneuvering by Senate Democrats and President Obama, a vote on New START would have been tabled until after the lame duck session, all but ensuring defeat of the treaty. Prior to New START, a bilateral nuclear arms control treaty with Russia had not received fewer than 80 votes; the average had been 88 votes.[15] Linton Brooks, former administrator of the Department of Energy's National Nuclear Security Administration, argues that the limited case history proves that party affiliation played a more dominant role in shaping opposition to New START than misgivings about the treaty's provisions. This suggests that the Obama administration's pursuit of a New START follow-on will encounter similar resistance. The declaration from Rose Gottemoeller, Acting Under Secretary of State for Arms Control and International Security, that "71 is the new 95" will be the new normal for as long as a Democrat serves as president.[16]

Contrasting New START to the 2003 Strategic Offensive Weapons Reduction Treaty (SORT) is illustrative, as both dealt with limits on strategic deployed weapons. The bare-bones three-page SORT document the Bush administration concluded with Russia was ratified by a 95–0 vote despite lacking any verification provisions. As Linton Brooks stated, "Republicans voted for it because George Bush signed it, and Democrats voted for it because while it may be poor arms control, it was arms control, and they like arms control."[17] Only one of the 24 Republicans who voted for SORT in 2003 backed New START seven years later, lending credence to the argument that criticism of the verification provisions in New START was, to some degree, influenced by domestic political considerations.[18]

Recommendation for Senate Ratification

As so much of the eventual U.S. domestic debate is condensed into sound bites, the Obama administration will need to justify any signed follow-on treaty to New START to senators and those who have influence over the ratification debate. Coordinated by the National Security Staff and involving the active participation of principals from the State, Defense, and Energy Departments, the persuasion offensive should emphasize the most compelling reasons to ratify a treaty. During floor debate the administration should reconstruct a

15. Arms Control Association, "U.S.-Russian Nuclear Arms Control Agreements at a Glance," August 2012, http://www.armscontrol.org/factsheets/USRussiaNuclearAgreementsMarch2010.

16. Senate Committee on Foreign Relations, *New START Implementation and Related Matters: Hearing Before the Committee on Foreign Relations*, 112th Congress, 2nd session, June 21, 2012.

17. Linton Brooks, telephone interview by author, Somerville, MA, December 15, 2012.

18. Walter Pincus, "New START: A similar arms reduction pact but a different Republican reaction," *Washington Post*, August 10, 2010, http://www.washingtonpost.com/wp-dyn/content/article/2010/08/09/AR2010080905461.html.

"war-room" in the U.S. Capitol to facilitate engagement and craft responses in real-time to assertions made by the opposition. Through office visits to targeted U.S. senators, public appearances, and Senate testimony, the administration must also maintain message discipline to prevent the opposition from exploiting inconsistencies to their advantage. The talking points should include:

- The follow-on treaty is not a "road to zero" in haste. President Obama's 2009 speech in Prague was aspirational. President John F. Kennedy's 1963 speech at American University contained the same language of an incremental disarmament conditioned on reciprocal steps taken by Russia. The remaining members of the five nuclear weapons states (as recognized by the Nuclear Non-Proliferation Treaty [NPT]) and the nuclear powers outside the NPT have explicitly stated that an additional round of U.S.-Russian reductions must occur before they make cuts to their own stockpiles.
- As with New START, verification would be a defining feature of the follow-on treaty. Failure to secure a treaty on NSNW means that the United States will continue to lack transparency on the location and movement of 2,000 or more nuclear warheads. A verification regime that permits U.S. inspectors into the different categories of Russian facilities will provide assurance of compliance with the treaty's deployed limits as well as proof of warhead destruction. When complemented by confidence building notifications and national technical means, the United States will be equipped to "trust but verify" nuclear reductions.
- NATO has fully concurred with reciprocal reductions with Russia. The alliance and U.S. commitment to collective security not only endures but is strengthened by withdrawing NSNW from Europe. With the future of the NATO nuclear mission jeopardized by fiscal and political pressures, the opportunity is fading to include NATO partners as part of a broad agreement. Further, a U.S. deterrent that prescribes a conventional military response to a crisis is far more credible than a nuclear response undertaken through the involvement of dual-use NATO aircraft.
- The Obama administration remains committed to modernization of the nuclear weapons complex, as evidenced by the unveiling of a FY 2014 budget request of $7.8 billion for the National Nuclear Security Administration's weapon activities, a 4 percent increase from the amount appropriated in the FY 2013 continuing resolution. Albeit below the figure pledged in the 2010 *Amended 1251 Report*, the fact that funding for weapons activities has increased in spite of constraints placed by the Budget Control Act shows President Obama's unwavering commitment to a safe, secure, and effective nuclear deterrent.[19]

19. Tom Collina, "Key Senator May Oppose New Treaties," *Arms Control Today* (July/August, 2012), http://www.armscontrol.org/2012_07-08/Key_Senator_May_Oppose_New_Treaties.

Conclusion

These policy recommendations are in response to the stated desire of the Obama administration to conclude a follow-on treaty to New START. A zone of possible agreement may exist if Russia expands lanes of cooperation with NATO and a treaty dually imposes limits on U.S. nondeployed strategic nuclear weapons and Russian nonstrategic nuclear weapons. The laborious but successful ratification of New START demonstrated that constructing a supermajority is possible even in the current era of politicized arms control policy. But the margin of error is small. The bloc of 71 votes that New START earned now has five fewer Democratic voters, and seven of the 13 Republicans who voted for the treaty are no longer in the U.S. Senate. Nonetheless, the elusive 67 vote mark can be reached if the administration can show its financial commitment to the nuclear weapons enterprise and can erect a coalition of supporters to offer counterpoints to inflammatory treaty critiques. To move beyond the Cold War legacy, U.S. and Russian leaders must muster the political will. An agreement that advances the interests of both states is not as elusive as it may seem.

Obstacles to a Middle East Nuclear-Weapon-Free Zone: Israel, Iran, and Beyond

Idon Natanzon[1]

Article VII of the Nuclear Non-Proliferation Treaty (NPT) stipulates that groups of states are free to conclude regional agreements banning nuclear weapons in clearly defined zones, known as nuclear-weapon-free zones (NWFZs).[2] Imposing strict guidelines on their members, five NWFZs currently encompass all of Latin America, Africa, and parts of Asia and the South Pacific,[3] mandating the removal of nuclear weapons from their territories, banning future use, and requiring verification and inspection standards. NWFZs have become an increasingly important aspect of the nonproliferation regime, and experts have heralded such agreements as important stepping stones toward global stability and security.

One region that continues to defy this trend is the Middle East. Rooted in deep-seeded religious, ethnic, and territorial conflicts, instability in the Middle East has been a near-constant reality. The advent of the nuclear age and subsequent proliferation has only inflamed these conflicts. With increasing tensions between Iran and Israel, instability in Iraq, the revolutions of the Arab Spring, the presence of international terrorist organizations, and the possibility of chemical and biological weapons use, stability in the Middle East cannot be guaranteed. Such concerns regarding stability in the Middle East has intensified international pressure to create a Middle East nuclear-weapon-free zone (MENFWZ). Yet, the member states of the Middle East remain frustratingly far from any such agreement. Two fundamental questions will be addressed. First, what are the major obstacles hindering the creation of a MENWFZ? Second, how likely is it that a MENWFZ can be established?

1. Idon Natanzon is a master's degree candidate at Johns Hopkins University's School of Advanced International Studies (SAIS).
2. Patricia Lewis, "A Middle East Free of Nuclear Weapons: Possible, Probable or Pipe-Dream?" *International Affairs* 89, no. 2 (2013): 437.
3. Ramesh Thakur, "Stepping Stones to a Nuclear-Weapon-Free World," in *Nuclear Weapons-Free Zones*, ed. Ramesh Thakur (New York: St. Martin's Press, 1998), 4.

The History of Nuclear-Weapon-Free Zones

NWFZs predate the NPT; both the Antarctic Treaty System (effective 1961) and the Outer Space Treaty[4] (effective 1967) contained agreements prohibiting nuclear weapon use years before the NPT was ratified in 1970.[5] The prospect of nuclear war between the United States and the Soviet Union created incentives for smaller states to establish regions free from nuclear weapons in order to protect themselves from the consequences of a nuclear conflict.[6] NWFZs became important milestones in broader arms control and are generally considered de facto "treaties for regional stability and confidence building."[7] While there is no consensus on the requirements of a NWFZ, they have developed cumulatively, as later agreements have built on the success of earlier arrangements.[8] There are five basic characteristics of a NWFZ: (1) the dismantlement of existing nuclear weapons; (2) the creation of restrictions against possessing or allowing the entry of nuclear weapons into the defined zone; (3) the abolition of the use or threat of use of nuclear weapons; (4) a prohibition on the possession of nuclear weapons for "peaceful purposes"; and (5) the establishment of standards for monitoring nuclear facilities and verifying compliance. A NWFZ, then, goes beyond the NPT and bans the possession, testing, deployment, or use of nuclear weapons in that zone.[9]

Establishing a Middle East Nuclear-Weapon-Free Zone

Prospects for a MENWFZ have been debated in international forums for over four decades; a proposal was officially adopted in the United Nations General Assembly in 1974. Confidence building measures within the proposal included urging all states to join the NPT, placing nuclear facilities under the watch of the International Atomic Energy Agency (IAEA), banning the testing and production of nuclear weapons, and agreeing that a MENWFZ would greatly increase regional and global stability.[10] Nearly all regional actors and all five of the nuclear weapons states voted in favor of the proposal; supporting proposals are adopted regularly, often by consensus. While Israel originally abstained, by 1980 it too had joined the consensus.[11]

In the early 1990s regional stability and comprehensive peace agreements between the Arab states and Israel appeared to be close at hand. Beginning in 1991 the Oslo peace

---

4. The formal name for this treaty is the Treaty on Principles Governing the Activities of States in the Exploration and Use of Outer Space, including the Moon and Other Celestial Bodies.

5. Thakur, "Stepping Stones to a Nuclear-Weapon-Free World," 4.

6. Gawdat Bahgat, *Proliferation of Nuclear Weapons* (Gainesville: University Press of Florida, 2007), 151.

7. Vilmos Cserveny, *Building a Weapons of Mass Destruction Free Zone in the Middle East: Global Non-Proliferation Regimes and Regional Experiences* (Geneva: UN Institute for Disarmament Research, 2004), 8.

8. Ibid., 8.

9. Ibid., 6–7.

10. Lewis, "A Middle East Free of Nuclear Weapons," 436.

11. Gerald M. Steinberg, "The Obstacles to a Middle East Nuclear-Weapon-Free Zone," in *Nuclear Weapons-Free Zones*, ed. Ramesh Thakur (New York: St. Martin's Press, 1998), 197.

process ushered in an unprecedented level of optimism, cooperation, and dialogue. The advancement of the peace process led many to believe that there was a growing potential for a MENWFZ.[12] Working groups such as Arms Control and Regional Security (ACRS) were established to discuss issues of regional stability, with the hope that members would reach agreement on a complete ban on all forms of weapons of mass destruction, whether they be nuclear, chemical, or biological.[13]

Throughout this brief period, a MENWFZ was "regarded as an entirely realistic, albeit lengthy project,"[14] with rival states making steady compromises on a number of core issues, including positive security guarantees from the nuclear weapons states and verification systems.[15] Working groups, such as ACRS, were viewed as lynchpin structures that could potentially lead to serious discussions of nuclear disarmament and a nuclear-weapon-free zone.[16] However, as the Oslo peace process failed to reach final status agreements, disillusionment ultimately fed into a new spiral of violence in the Middle East. Concurrently, members of the ACRS grew increasingly frustrated with the lack of progress being made, especially with regard to a MENWFZ.

During the 1995 NPT renewal conference, Middle Eastern states demanded a specific reference to a MENWFZ.[17] While the provision was included, the issue was not revisited for the next 10 years and a MENWFZ proposal did not resurface on the international agenda until 2010. Currently new regional forums are being established[18] and a Middle East Conference was scheduled to take place (but ultimately postponed indefinitely) in Finland in 2012.[19] It is unclear whether the conference would have been successful, as Israel had already opted out of attending and tensions between Iran and the other Middle East states remain high. Despite these impediments, both Israel and the Arab/Muslim states continue to support positions in favor of a weapon-of-mass-destruction-free zone (WMDFZ).[20] Whether this is merely empty rhetoric or a true commitment to the pursuit of a Middle East free of weapons of mass destruction remains to be seen. Even with overwhelming regional and global support, a MENWFZ remains stubbornly out of reach, progress appears permanently stalled,[21] and a multitude of obstacles have curtailed the creation of a NWFZ.

---

12. Shai Feldman, *Nuclear Weapons and Arms Control in the Middle East* (Cambridge, MA: MIT Press, 1997), 1.
13. Dalia Dassa Kaye, "The Middle East WMD-Free Zone Conference," *Nonproliferation Review* 19, no. 3 (2012): 416.
14. Ivan Trushkin, "WMD-Free Zone in the Middle East: From Ideas to Reality," *Security Index: A Russian Journal on International Security* 17, no. 4 (2011): 58.
15. Ibid.
16. Lewis, "A Middle East Free of Nuclear Weapons," 438.
17. Vladimir Orlov, "A Nuclear-Weapon-Free Middle East: Looking for Solutions," *International Affairs: A Russian Journal of World Politics, Diplomacy & International Relations* 57, no. 4 (2011): 2.
18. Trushkin, "WMD-Free Zone in the Middle East," 62.
19. Lewis, "A Middle East Free of Nuclear Weapons," 442.
20. Kaye, "The Middle East WMD-Free Zone Conference," 417.
21. Cserveny, *Building a Weapons of Mass Destruction Free Zone in the Middle East*, 90.

Obstacles to a Nuclear-Weapon-Free Middle East

Given the current conditions of the Middle East, a MENWFZ might appear impossible. The region is host to a variety of obstacles: a lack of regional harmony, the absence of effective regional organizations, instability, sectarian violence, the broader Arab-Israeli conflict, and the rising threat of a nuclear-armed Iran. Further, any efforts must address great challenges associated with an assumed Israeli nuclear arsenal.[22] Nevertheless, giving up on such a proposal would be unwise. The nonproliferation regime is at a crossroads; international institutions must continue to encourage regional processes and principal actors must find a way to bridge the palpable differences between them in order to ensure regional and global stability.

Perhaps the most obvious obstacle to a MENWFZ is a semantic one. Critical to any NWFZ are clearly defined and recognized borders, yet concretely defining what countries are included in the "Middle East" is more of a political undertaking than a geographical one.[23] The Middle East is not afforded with regional isolation or separation due to natural barriers, and no genuine regional hegemon exists. Countries such as Saudi Arabia, Egypt, and Iran each have their own spheres of influence, and Israel, although universally considered to have the strongest military, is virtually isolated from regional decisionmaking structures. Further, the refusal of many Arab and Muslim states to formally recognize Israel's existence[24] poses another unique challenge. Based in a religious-territorial conflict, many of these states abstain from establishing any formal relations with the Jewish state, and Israel remains largely isolated.[25] Even working groups such as the ACRS were boycotted by certain key Arab states such as Syria and Lebanon.[26]

Any NWFZ negotiations that exclude Israel will be an exercise in futility.[27] A MENWFZ would need to include not only Israel, the region's sole nuclear-armed state, but also all Arab League countries, Iran, North Africa, and perhaps even Turkey and Afghanistan[28]—states that are not currently part of the IAEA definition of the Middle East. [29] Such an arrangement would be both inclusive and comprehensive, more accurately reflecting the political, social, and regional dynamics of the Greater Middle East. In a Middle Eastern context, taking these considerations into account is more vital to the success of a MENWFZ than the strict geographical definition of the region.

---

22. Ibrahim A. Karawan, "The Case for a Nuclear-Weapon-Free Zone in the Middle East," in *Nuclear Weapons-Free Zones*, ed. Ramesh Thakur (New York: St. Martin's Press, 1998), 184.
23. Cserveny, *Building a Weapons of Mass Destruction Free Zone in the Middle East*, 108.
24. Steinberg, "The Obstacles to a Middle East Nuclear-Weapon-Free Zone," 195.
25. Ibid.
26. Feldman, *Nuclear Weapons and Arms Control in the Middle East*, 208.
27. Mahmoud Karem, *A Nuclear-Weapon-Free Zone in the Middle East* (Westport, CT: Greenwood Press, 1988), 64.
28. Steinberg, "The Obstacles to a Middle East Nuclear-Weapon-Free Zone," 196.
29. Officially, the IAEA definition for the Middle East spans the area east-to-west from Iran to Libya and north-to-south from Syria to Yemen, excluding states such as Sudan, Turkey, Afghanistan, and Pakistan. See Cserveny, *Building a Weapons of Mass Destruction Free Zone in the Middle East*, 108.

The Middle East, unlike other regions, lacks any inclusive and comprehensive "multilateral institution within which to explore and advance the zone concept."[30] Subregional groups such as the Gulf Cooperation Council, the Organization of the Petroleum Exporting Countries, and even the Arab League are ill-equipped to initiate such negotiations.[31] Yet, some experts still cling to the working group structures of the Oslo period and believe that reinvigorating groups such as the ACRS could lead to a credible and "serious venue for discussing and negotiating arms control."[32] Such an arrangement would compensate for the absence of any true regional hegemon; however, new working groups would still require the participation of states such as Syria and Lebanon, both of which did not participate in the 1990s.[33]

Each of these obstacles feeds into the general sense of disharmony in the region—a region home to a complicated web of adversarial relationships and powerful non-state actors.[34] Tensions exist between Israel and most regional actors; traditionally Shi'a and Sunni countries; Muslims and other religious or ethnic minorities such as Christians, Berbers, and Kurds; terrorist organizations such as Hezbollah and al Qaeda; and between religious moderates, extremists, and secular Muslims. Coupled with the recent protests and revolutions, popularly known as the Arab Spring, the Middle East is perhaps more fractured today than at any other moment in its past.

Undoubtedly, Israel, and the uncertainty surrounding its nuclear arsenal, remains the most salient regional pressure point. Officially, Israel has adopted a policy of ambiguity or opacity with regard to its alleged nuclear arsenal, commonly known in Hebrew as *amimut*.[35] Instead of choosing a nuclear policy of resolve (proliferation) or caution (nonproliferation), Israel has combined the two into a nuclear strategy that both deters its rivals but leaves a great deal of uncertainty.[36] From its establishment, the development of Israel's nuclear program was seen as central to the country's national defense. The state began seeking the tools and resources to implement a nuclear weapons program by the early 1950s; by the mid-1960s Central Intelligence Agency reports indicate that Israel was already believed to be a nuclear-armed state.[37] Yet even after the 1986 revelation by Mordechai Vanunu, an Israeli nuclear technician-turned-whistleblower, Israel's policy of *amimut* persists and Israeli leaders refuse to confirm or deny any nuclear-weapon-related activity. Working closely with the United States, Israel recognizes that it can remain an exemption to the nonproliferation regime as long as it "keeps its weapons invisible"[38] and does not test or threaten to use its apparently vast nuclear arsenal.[39]

30. Kaye, "The Middle East WMD-Free Zone Conference," 414.
31. Thakur, "Stepping Stones to a Nuclear-Weapon-Free World," 29.
32. Feldman, *Nuclear Weapons and Arms Control in the Middle East*, 14.
33. Ibid., 208.
34. Kaye, "The Middle East WMD-Free Zone Conference," 414.
35. Avner Cohen, *The Worst Kept Secret: Israel's Bargain with the Bomb* (New York: Columbia University Press, 2010), xi.
36. Ibid., 39.
37. Feldman, *Nuclear Weapons and Arms Control in the Middle East*, 43–44.
38. Cohen, *The Worst Kept Secret*, xxxi.
39. Karawan, "The Case for a Nuclear-Weapon-Free Zone in the Middle East," 185.

Forty years later, despite never testing a nuclear weapon,[40] Israel has yet to sign the NPT but has similarly tried not to outright reject it. *Amimut* requires Israel to balance nonproliferation norms with its own security,[41] and Israel has intervened militarily when others appeared close to producing nuclear weapons. In response to Israel's nuclear program, rival states have sought to (1) acquire their own nuclear weapons; (2) stockpile chemical and/or biological weapons; (3) maintain a military balance of power; and (4) exert considerable diplomatic pressure through international institutions for Israel to dismantle its program.[42] While Israel's position links nuclear weapons to deterrence in order to balance numerical asymmetries, Israel's opponents see a nuclear Israel much more cynically. They believe that Israel has acquired nuclear weapons to compel Arab states, to embarrass the Arab people, and to highlight Arab strategic inferiority.

Despite these fundamentally opposed perspectives, Israeli nuclear weapons have not exacerbated tensions in the Middle East, and opacity has actually moderated some Arab ambitions to acquire nuclear weapons. Israel has proven to be a prudent nuclear-armed state and "by not publicly flaunting its nuclear status, Israel has reduced its neighbors' incentives to proliferate."[43] While there is some evidence suggesting that Israel contemplated using tactical nuclear weapons during the early stages of the 1973 Arab-Israeli War,[44] it refrained from doing so. It has not made a significant nuclear threat in decades.[45] Yet this tension has proven to be one of the most debilitating obstacles to a MENWFZ. Israel's nuclear arsenal would have to be addressed prior to any meaningful discussions of a NWFZ.[46] Unfortunately, many experts believe that Israel will never give up its nuclear arsenal even with guarantees of a comprehensive MENWFZ, and the program is widely popular in Israel, as nearly 90 percent of Israelis "explicitly approve of the continuation of Israeli nuclear policy."[47]

While Israel is committed to retaining its nuclear weapons monopoly in the Middle East, demonstrated through military strikes against Iraq and Syria, the greatest current threat concerns Iran. Iran has pursued nuclear technology since the 1950s and has maintained a civilian nuclear program since the 1960s.[48] Yet it has recently intensified its efforts and is believed to have been pursuing nuclear weapons for nearly two decades.[49] Iran's proliferation poses significant challenges to both Israel and the broader region, as the threat of a nuclear arms race may spur Iran's regional rivals such as Saudi Arabia and even Egypt to pursue their own nuclear programs.[50] Such violations of the NPT may alter the foreign policy strategies of other regional actors, including the Gulf states. With those conditions,

---

40. Avner Cohen, *Israel and the Bomb* (New York: Columbia University Press, 1998), 299–300.
41. Feldman, *Nuclear Weapons and Arms Control in the Middle East*, 98.
42. Gawdat Bahgat, "A WMD-Free Zone in the Middle East?" *Middle East Policy* 20, no. 1 (2013): 32.
43. Avner Cohen and Marvin Miller, "Bringing Israel's Bomb Out of the Basement: Has Nuclear Ambiguity Outlived Its Shelf Life?" *Foreign Affairs* 89, no. 5 (2010): 36.
44. Karem, *A Nuclear-Weapon-Free Zone in the Middle East*, 93.
45. Cohen, *Israel and the Bomb*, 342.
46. Thakur, "Stepping Stones to a Nuclear-Weapon-Free World," 29.
47. Steinberg, "The Obstacles to a Middle East Nuclear-Weapon-Free Zone," 203.
48. Feldman, *Nuclear Weapons and Arms Control in the Middle East*, 49.
49. Bahgat, *Proliferation of Nuclear Weapons*, 147.
50. Cohen, *The Worst Kept Secret*, 221.

Turkey could also entertain nuclear aspirations, posing a real proliferation threat at Europe's doorstep. Nuclear weapons could further embolden Iran, setting the stage for a more aggressive Iranian foreign policy and a more adventurous military strategy in the region.[51]

In response, international efforts have led to an impressive sanctions regime against the Iranian government.[52] Some Gulf states now view a nuclear Iran as an even greater obstacle to a MENWFZ than Israel.[53] Others in the Arab world remain divided, since an Iranian bomb might establish Muslim parity with the Jewish state.[54] Despite the ongoing debate, Iran vehemently "denies that it is pursuing a nuclear-weapons capability and insists that its nuclear program solely aims at meeting its growing civilian energy needs."[55] International efforts to negotiate with Iran have repeatedly failed.[56] Nevertheless, a consensus has formed in the international community that "at the least, Iran wants to come very close to the nuclear-weapons threshold by maintaining a large-scale enrichment capability" and keeping a level of secrecy over the status of its nuclear weapon development.[57] While Iran appears to be attempting to mimic Israel's policy of opacity, Israeli officials refuse to accept any similarities between the two programs and view a nuclear Iran as an existential danger, repeatedly threatening that military strikes to destroy Iran's facilities remain a possibility.[58]

These tensions between Israel, Iran, and the Arab states highlight an important challenge to a MENWFZ. Will a MENWFZ instill regional trust leading to comprehensive peace settlements between Israel and the Arab/Muslim world, or does such an agreement need to be in place to ensure Israel's safety before a MENWFZ can be negotiated? This issue of sequencing has thus far allowed each side to support a MENWFZ in theory while they reject the practical steps needed to implement one. Many believe that the 2002 Arab peace initiative, which promised Israel normalized relations with the members of the Arab League in exchange for a resolution to the Arab-Israeli conflict, would be the most appropriate launching point for any significant regional agreement. Yet, in order for Israel to feel secure enough to dismantle its nuclear arsenal, the Arab peace initiative would need to be agreed upon prior to arms negotiations, and similar agreements would need to be reached with non–Arab League countries such as Iran,[59] scenarios that have already been rejected.

The Middle East faces additional challenges from non-state actors such as transnational terrorist organizations. In the post-9/11 world, such actors are increasingly believed to be "in the market for radioactive materials." Further, the expansion of a nuclear black market

51. Ibid., 220–221.
52. Lewis, "A Middle East Free of Nuclear Weapons," 449.
53. Bahgat, "A WMD-Free Zone in the Middle East?" 34.
54. Mohamed ElBaradei, *The Age of Deception: Nuclear Diplomacy in Treacherous Times* (New York: Metropolitan Books, 2011), 223.
55. Bahgat, "A WMD-Free Zone in the Middle East?" 35.
56. Steven E. Miller, "Nuclear Weapons 2011: Momentum Slows, Reality Returns," *Bulletin of the Atomic Scientists* 68, no. 1 (2012): 24.
57. Cohen, *The Worst Kept Secret*, 228.
58. Ibid., 236.
59. Cserveny, *Building a Weapons of Mass Destruction Free Zone in the Middle East*, 18.

has been a growing concern for intelligence agencies[60] seeking to prevent a non-state actor or a country from importing a "quick fix nuclear capability."[61] While the possibility of a non-state actor acquiring nuclear weapons remains minimal, Middle Eastern governments continue to be vigilant against the spread of fissile materials and global powers are trying to take actions to limit the spread of so-called loose-nukes.[62]

Finally, there are logistical impediments to a successful MENWFZ. First, a robust verification system with the power to identify and punish violators has not been agreed upon. Beyond Israel's non-NPT status, the region has been host to a variety of known transgressors such as Syria, Iraq, Libya, and Iran.[63] Israel's military interventions have stymied the spread of nuclear weapons[64]; however, such actions are in many ways counterproductive to regional stability. While there have been several recommendations for verification systems—including one based on reciprocal verification, another leveraging established structures in the IAEA, or even another using Interpol[65]—none have satisfied the principal actors. Second, there is a growing interest in civilian nuclear energy.[66] Countries throughout the region (most recently the United Arab Emirates) now view nuclear power as a sustainable alternative to their traditional energy forms. While civilian nuclear use is allowed under the NPT, the further spread of nuclear technologies in a region with known previous violators of the NPT (namely Syria, Libya, and Iran) could pose potential threats. Finally, a MENWFZ is hampered by the region's inability to agree on which weapons should be banned, as some experts maintain that an agreement must include the massive chemical and biological weapons stockpiles present in the region.[67] To date, attempts to expand a NWFZ to a WMDFZ have been met with significant backlash from many regional actors.

Outlook and Recommendations

Any successful MENWFZ will have to balance individual security interests while taking into account global responsibility and disarmament. While the status quo is untenable, particularly with the rapidly changing dynamics in the Middle East, neither Israel nor the Arab/Muslim states seem willing to shift their entrenched positions. Yet, there may still be room for optimism, as all parties have expressed support for the theoretical framework of a NWFZ. While each state may approach national security differently and some may have differing views concerning the future of the region, each government has an obligation to its own citizens to ensure a safe and secure Middle East. This simple convergence of interests must be the foundation for any MENWFZ.

60. ElBaradei, *The Age of Deception*, 164.
61. Feldman, *Nuclear Weapons and Arms Control in the Middle East*, 39.
62. Lewis, "A Middle East Free of Nuclear Weapons," 433–435.
63. Kaye, "The Middle East WMD-Free Zone Conference," 415.
64. Cohen, *The Worst Kept Secret*, xxi.
65. Adam Zarazinski, "Steps to a Nuclear Weapons Free Zone in the Middle East," *Defense Monitor* 40, no. 4 (2011): 5.
66. Bahgat, "A WMD-Free Zone in the Middle East?" 30.
67. Cserveny, *Building a Weapons of Mass Destruction Free Zone in the Middle East*, 32.

The postponement of the 2012 Middle East conference represents a missed opportunity for both the region and the global nonproliferation regime. While instability remains as a result of the Arab Spring, getting the principal actors to restart negotiations under a framework similar to the ACRS of the Oslo period will be critical. In the absence of strong regional institutions, influential outside parties such as the United States must reinforce such initiatives and encourage all parties to participate instead of passively allowing such opportunities to deflate.[68] Yet even a Middle East conference on nuclear disarmament will not untangle the complex web of conflicts in the region. Tensions between Sunni and Shi'a Muslims, Israel and its rivals, and others will continue. Further work must therefore be dedicated to reducing the general level of hostility and distrust in the region.

While a genuine NWFZ might not be realistic in the foreseeable future, a wide variety of confidence building measures (CBMs) must be enacted to prepare for the conditions necessary for a MENWFZ. Of the many proposals for CBMs the most salient include:

1. A comprehensive no-first-use policy in the region
2. Refraining from attacking other countries' nuclear facilities (including using cyber capabilities)
3. Incentivizing Israel to make its official position of no-first-use legally binding[69]
4. Banning the production of fissile materials in the region[70]
5. Setting a cap on all forms of weapons of mass destruction (WMD) stockpiles in the region
6. Placing all nuclear facilities under IAEA (or other international) monitoring[71]
7. Agreeing to other arms-control treaties such as the Comprehensive Test Ban Treaty[72] and/or the Fissile Materials Cutoff Treaty[73]
8. Strengthening relationships between Middle Eastern countries through inclusive regional institutions and economic partnerships[74]

As a set, these CBMs represent an ambitious plan for the Middle East. Any combination of such "first steps" would significantly impact the region. Importantly, the negotiation of CBMs builds confidence itself. Just as the ACRS structure failed to bring progress in the 1990s,[75] so too could this new set of CBMs be insufficient without full regional cooperation. Middle Eastern states must therefore identify common interests among adversaries. While there remain a variety of obstacles to achieving a NWFZ, progress must nevertheless push

68. Miller, "Nuclear Weapons 2011," 26.
69. Karem, *A Nuclear-Weapon-Free Zone in the Middle East*, 126.
70. Feldman, *Nuclear Weapons and Arms Control in the Middle East*, 284.
71. Trushkin, "WMD-Free Zone in the Middle East," 56.
72. Orlov, "A Nuclear Weapon-Free Middle East," 8.
73. Cohen, *The Worst Kept Secret*, 233.
74. Karem, *A Nuclear-Weapon-Free Zone in the Middle East*, 121.
75. Kaye, "The Middle East WMD-Free Zone Conference," 423.

forward and begin to address both Israel's security concerns as well as the Arab/Muslim world's threat perception of Israel's nuclear arsenal.

Despite the many challenges, some have argued that "the prospects for a NWFZ are not as grim as they once seemed."[76] First, there are currently no operational military pacts in the region that provide nuclear umbrellas to any country in the Middle East. Whereas a NWFZ in other regions would be complicated by such a factor, the Middle East does not need to worry about such matters.[77] Second, North African states can help lead the way toward a MENWFZ, as they are already signatories to the African nuclear-weapon-free zone[78] (member states who have not yet ratified the treaty should do so as an additional CBM). Finally, and perhaps most importantly, all parties have already agreed in principle to the idea of a MENWFZ. While this may be dismissed by some as mere political gesturing, it is a vital first step toward any successful NWFZ. Even Israel, the singular nuclear-armed state in the region, has intermittently shown some openness to such an idea.

Regional parties and international actors must continue to advance CBMs and incentivize one another to participate. Progress must be made in the Arab-Israeli conflict, as MENWFZ negotiations will require all parties to officially acknowledge one another. Credible third parties must take leadership roles in the absence of effective regional institutions. Ultimately, progress toward a comprehensive and inclusive MENWFZ will require creativity, sacrifice, and a great deal of trust from all parties involved.[79] In doing so, each country will have to reassess its longstanding sociopolitical positions. While a MENWFZ may seem impossible, its alternative—the potential for widespread nuclear proliferation—is unsustainable.[80]

---

76. Zarazinski, "Steps to a Nuclear Weapons Free Zone in the Middle East," 3.
77. Karem, *A Nuclear-Weapon-Free Zone in the Middle East*, 123.
78. Zarazinski, "Steps to a Nuclear Weapons Free Zone in the Middle East," 4.
79. Cohen, *The Worst Kept Secret*, 237.
80. ElBaradei, *The Age of Deception*, 321.

The Non-State Actor Threat to Pakistan's Nuclear Weapons

Jonathan Papp[1]

The *Global Trends 2030: Alternative Worlds* report by the National Intelligence Council describes the value of nuclear weapons to states, stating, "Nuclear powers such as Russia and Pakistan and potential aspirants such as Iran and North Korea see nuclear weapons as compensation for other political and security weaknesses, heightening the risk of their use."[2] Scholars have reasoned that, as nuclear weapons proliferate, the probability of a nuclear detonation by either a state or non-state actor will increase.[3] This argument is sensible; more weapons increase the probability that a safety mechanism could fail and increase the number of opportunities that a non-state actor could have to acquire a nuclear weapon. While each state has its own standards and safety regulations, even high standards can be compromised. Out of all nuclear states, Pakistan is often cited as the foremost concern, given the state's precarious relationship with violent Islamist groups. However, this concern is misplaced. The United States has fixated on Pakistan's nuclear base security when policy-makers should be more concerned with nuclear components outside of secured facilities.

Security of Weapons in Military Facilities

THE KAMRA AIR BASE ATTACKS

Pakistan's nuclear arsenal has been portrayed as a continual worry in the U.S. media, despite U.S. government efforts to downplay the threat.[4] This worry was exacerbated by the torrent of stories questioning the security of Pakistani nuclear stockpiles after a group of Taliban fighters attacked Kamra Air Base in August 2012. The attacks were concerning because the base long had been suspected of housing nuclear weapons[5]—a charge the

1. Jonathan Papp is a graduate of the Graduate School of Public and International Affairs at the University of Pittsburgh. In the summer of 2013, he worked as a research intern at the CSIS Project on Nuclear Issues. The views expressed here do not necessarily reflect those of CSIS or the Project on Nuclear Issues.

2. National Intelligence Council, *Global Trends 2030: Alternative Worlds,* NIC 2012-001 (Washington, DC: U.S. Government Printing Office, 2013), 16.

3. Sidney D. Drell, "The Gravest Danger: Nuclear Weapons and Their Proliferation," in *Two Cultures: Essays in Honour of David Speiser*, ed. Kim Williams (Basel, Switzerland: Birkhäuser Basel, 2006), 182–183.

4. Associated Press, "Clinton downplays threat to Pakistan nuke arsenal," *Sydney Morning Herald*, October 12, 2009, http://www.smh.com.au/world/clinton-downplays-threat-to-pakistan-nuke-arsenal-20091012-gsk2.html.

5. "Gunmen storm military air base in Pakistan," BBC News, August 16, 2012, http://www.bbc.co.uk/news/world-asia-19278302.

Pakistani military has consistently denied.[6] Whether or not Kamra houses nuclear weapons, the threat of the attack by the Taliban militants was wildly overblown.

The logic that a Taliban attack on an air force base constitutes a threat to the entire Pakistani nuclear arsenal requires more rigorous analysis. First, the attackers were wearing suicide vests when they breached the base's security perimeter. The presence of suicide vests indicates they did not plan to leave the base alive. Second, if the Taliban fighters were planning to recover nuclear material or any substantial military equipment, they would have sent more than a nine-man team to attack a heavily guarded Pakistani military base. Logistically, it would be difficult for nine men to transport a nuclear warhead without knowing the exact locations of the weapons. Infiltrating the base's perimeter is a much different proposition than gaining access to and exfiltrating material or equipment from a base. Shashindra Tyagi, a former chief of staff of the Indian Air Force sums up the concerns by stating, "All of the steps that could be taken have been taken. This business of the Taliban taking over—it can't be ruled out, but I think it's unlikely. The Pakistani military understands the threats they face better than anyone, and they are smart enough to take care of it."[7]

COMMAND AND CONTROL

Yuri Korolev, a member of the Russian Foreign Ministry, expressed concern about non-state actors in Pakistan, stating, "There are 120,000–130,000 people directly involved in Pakistan's nuclear and missile programs. . . . There is no way to guarantee that all are 100 [percent] loyal and reliable."[8] While Korolev is correct to question the reliability of all the nuclear-related workers in Pakistan, the Pakistanis have also implemented safeguards and have shown an increasing interest in working with the United States to implement them.[9] The improvements in nuclear security are not a cure-all, but they demonstrate that high-level Pakistani policymakers are serious about addressing security concerns.

Pakistan employs adequate mechanisms to ensure the safety of its nuclear arsenal and has actively reformed the institutions charged with this task. The government of Pakistan has continually pointed out that warheads are kept separate from detonation mechanisms and warhead cores separate from their firing mechanisms. Keeping the components separate limits the ability of non-state actors to possess an operational weapon after a potential compromise and increases the number of materials a non-state actor would need to obtain

6. Alex Rodriguez, "Attack on Pakistan base raises fear about nuclear arsenal," *Los Angeles Times*, August 16, 2012, http://latimesblogs.latimes.com/world_now/2012/08/raid-on-air-force-base-raises-fears-about-pakistans-nuclear-arsenal-security.html.

7. Tom Hundley, "Pakistan and India: Race to the End," Pulitzer Center, September 5, 2012, http://pulitzercenter.org/reporting/pakistan-nuclear-weapons-battlefield-india-arms-race-energy-cold-war.

8. David Leigh, "WikiLeaks cables expose Pakistan nuclear fears," *The Guardian*, November 30, 2010, http://www.guardian.co.uk/world/2010/nov/30/wikileaks-cables-pakistan-nuclear-fears.

9. David E. Sanger and William J. Broad, "U.S. Secretly Aids Pakistan in Guarding Nuclear Weapons," *New York Times*, November 18, 2007.

in order to acquire a functional nuclear warhead and delivery vehicle.[10] Pakistan has also instituted a permissive action link (PAL) system, strikingly similar to the system the United States utilizes.[11] As part of the PAL system, two members of the military as well as the most senior civilian leaders have codes that must be entered simultaneously to approve the use of strategic nuclear weapons or the deployment of tactical battlefield nuclear weapons.[12]

Pakistan has reformed its institutions in an attempt to mirror internationally accepted standards of nuclear security in storage facilities. The security and safety of Pakistan's nuclear force rely on three institutions: the National Command Authority (NCA), the Strategic Plans Division, and the Strategic Forces Commands. The NCA is significant, because the final authorization to employ a nuclear weapon must go through the chair of the NCA or the current prime minister. The director general of the army is the secretariat for the NCA, and each branch of the military has its own Strategic Forces Command.[13] This provides Pakistan with a multitier approach to prevent an accidental launch. In addition, Pakistan has developed a personnel reliability program to scrutinize individuals working with nuclear weapons in Pakistan. While there remains the possibility of individuals within the nuclear establishment aiding non-state actors in obtaining a nuclear device, institutional controls on the arsenal have improved. These safety efforts reflect Pakistani priorities in securing the arsenal.

Vulnerable Weapons

DISPERSAL STRATEGY

While Pakistan's current arsenal appears relatively secure, this reality may not persist indefinitely. Due to security fears, there is a possibility that Pakistan will adopt a strategy of spreading out its nuclear weapons. If the storage of weapons becomes more spread out, the security at nuclear weapon storage depots will likely be degraded, since the number of sites to be protected will increase, requiring the same resources to protect a greater number of facilities.

WEAPONS ON THE MOVE

A joint project by *The Atlantic* and *National Journal* found that Pakistan has begun transporting nuclear weapons in civilian vehicles, which suggests that the security of

10. Peter Crail, "Pakistani Nuclear Stocks Safe, Officials Say," *Arms Control Today* (June 2009), 29, http://www.armscontrol.org/act/2009_6/Pakistan.

11. Gordon Corera, "Pakistan's political crisis has raised a number of troubling questions—could the state collapse, could militants come to power, could the country's nuclear arms fall into the wrong hands?," BBC, February 4, 2013, http://news.bbc.co.uk/2/hi/south_asia/7225175.stm.

12. Zafar Nawaz Jaspal, "Pakistan's nuclear weapons safety and security," *The Nation*, February 23, 2013, http://www.nation.com.pk/pakistan-news-newspaper-daily-english-online/columns/23-Feb-2013/pakistan-s-nuclear-weapons-safety-and-security.

13. Kenneth N. Luongo and Naeem Salik, "Building Confidence in Pakistan's Nuclear Security," *Arms Control Today* (December 2007), http://www.armscontrol.org/act/2007_12/Luongo.

the nuclear arsenal is worse than currently believed.[14] The evidence for the worrisome transportation methods is based on the authors' interviews conducted over a six month period. Pakistani government officials have expressed concern regarding improving relations between the United States and India, worrying that these warmer ties indicate the United States' intention to "side" with India in potential disputes.[15] The Pakistani military worries that the United States is sharing intelligence on Pakistani nuclear forces with India. Transporting assembled nuclear weapons in civilian vehicles may become common practice as a way to avoid detection by Indian and U.S. intelligence.[16]

DEPLOYMENT OF WEAPONS

A conceivable scenario has been put forth by Michael Krepon, co-founder of the Stimson Center and director of its South Asia and Space Security programs. He writes, "Another compelling reason against military [mobilization] is that [it] would likely place more of Pakistan's nuclear assets in motion, where they would be less well protected against domestic enemies of the state."[17] Security has increased on military bases, despite the media's attention on attacks by various groups near bases purported to house nuclear weapons. The larger worry is that increasing tensions between Pakistan and India will cause Pakistan to deploy tactical nuclear weapons in an attempt to deter an invasion by superior Indian conventional forces. There are indications that both India and Pakistan increased their nuclear alert levels and mated nuclear warheads to trigger mechanisms during the 1999 Kargil War.[18] There exists a much higher probability that non-state actors will target nuclear forces once deployed. As a result, a rise in the tensions between India and Pakistan increases the threat of a compromised nuclear weapon.

U.S. Policy Moving Forward

The United States must continue to engage Pakistan on nuclear weapons security. While the United States has provided a vast amount of aid to Pakistan, the amount devoted to improving the safety of Pakistan's nuclear arsenal is unclear. Still, some public information on cooperation is available. For example, the United States worked with Pakistan to build a nuclear security training center[19] and provided a large amount of aid to increase the physical security of nuclear weapon storage facilities.[20] While physical security improvements

14. Jeffrey Goldberg and Marc Ambinder, "The Ally from Hell," *The Atlantic*, October 28, 2011, http://www.theatlantic.com/magazine/archive/2011/12/the-ally-from-hell/308730/4/.

15. "Pakistan Command Meeting Voices Concern Over Indo-US Nuclear Deal," Pakistan TV, April 12, 2006.

16. Seymour M. Hersh, "Defending the Arsenal: In an unstable Pakistan, can nuclear warheads be kept safe?" *New* Yorker, November 16, 2009, http://www.newyorker.com/reporting/2009/11/16/091116fa_fact_hersh?currentPage=all.

17. Michael Krepon, "Complexities of nuclear risk reduction in South Asia," *The Hindu*, May 29, 2009, http://www.hindu.com/2009/05/29/stories/2009052954910900.htm.

18. Hundley, "Pakistan and India."

19. David E. Sanger and William J. Broad, "U.S. Secretly Aids Pakistan in Guarding Nuclear Weapons," *New York Times*, November 18, 2007, http://www.nytimes.com/2007/11/18/washington/18nuke.html?pagewanted=all&_r=0.

20. Ibid.

are progressing, the United States also needs to focus on the larger security concerns of Pakistan.

One of Pakistan's security concerns is based on a fear that U.S. and Indian intelligence agencies will successfully identify and track components of Pakistan's nuclear arsenal.[21] Funding from the United States to improve security on bases in any amount will not solve the underlying problems that are causing Pakistan to transport components using civilian vehicles. Further, the prospects for solving the problem of unsecured transportation of nuclear materials are remote, given that the United States' relationship with India is the principle reason for this new strategy.

It is difficult for the United States to completely allay Pakistan's fears, but it can take some steps to improve the situation. The first problem is that too much focus, time, and thought has been dedicated to thinking about ways to secure weapons stored on bases. Instead, U.S. policymakers should devote substantial intellectual capital to thinking of new ways to convince Pakistan to securely transport its nuclear materials; policymakers cannot solve a problem they do not acknowledge. One possible option for the United States is to help Pakistan design a kill switch or another measure capable of disabling a device if a weapon component leaves its transport vehicle.

Building trust between Pakistan and India will address the reasons why Pakistan risks transporting nuclear materials in unsecured vehicles. The United States should act as a broker to foster dialogue between Pakistan and India as part of a long-term strategy. The U.S. government has shown a willingness to vocalize its wishes to reduce tensions in the region, exemplified by Secretary of State John Kerry's remarks in a recent 2013 visit to India.[22] The return to office of Prime Minister Nawaz Sharif in Pakistan also brings forth renewed hope that relations will improve.[23] The United States should promote public diplomacy and continue to call for an improvement in relations between India and Pakistan. The Obama administration should focus on improving relations through areas of mutual interest, including with regard to funding security measures for the reliable and safe transportation of nuclear components. These measures do not serve as a silver bullet for solving Pakistan's nuclear security problems, but they will help reduce tensions in the region.

Conclusion

On the one hand, Pakistan's military bases have increased their physical security, and Pakistan has restructured its institutions to create a multilayered approach to nuclear security. On the other hand, Pakistan has allegedly started transporting nuclear components in civilian vehicles, a practice that vastly increases the threat posed by non-state

21. Goldberg and Ambinder, "The Ally From Hell."

22. "US wants India to improve relations with Pakistan," *Daily Times*, June 27, 2013, http://www.dailytimes.com.pk/default.asp?page=2013\06\27\story_27-6-2013_pg4_8.

23. Rahul Kansal, "Nawaz Sharif's coming to power is an opportunity India must not miss," *The Times of India*, June 21, 2013, http://articles.timesofindia.indiatimes.com/2013-06-21/edit-page/40118744_1_nawaz-sharif-pakistani-taliban-bilateral-relationship.

actors. While continuing to engage Pakistan by sharing best practices and funding nuclear storage facility security, the United States should refocus the emphasis of its efforts on addressing the threat of non-state actor theft of a weapon when outside secure facilities. If the United States wants to protect the Pakistani nuclear arsenal against true threats to international security, then it should focus on developing strategies to convince Pakistan that transporting unsecured nuclear weapons creates unnecessary vulnerabilities that non-state actors can exploit. It is in the long-term interest of the United States to aid in building trust between Pakistan and India to end irresponsible transportation practices that leave all parties vulnerable to a compromised nuclear weapon.

Ballistic Missile Defense and the Iranian Threat: Key Issues

Raj Pattani[1]

This essay provides an overview of issues associated with ballistic missile defense (BMD), with a specific emphasis on the ability of the United States to defend against Iranian ballistic missiles.[2] This discussion does not seek to explore the broader strategic implications of BMD; it seeks only to find ways to make the U.S. BMD architecture more effective in performing the limited defensive missions articulated by the Obama administration. The overview proceeds with an explanation of BMD concepts, a description of Iran's ballistic missile capabilities, a summary of the current BMD program of the United States, and a survey of critiques of the BMD program. High-level recommendations close the discussion.

Ballistic Missile Defense Concepts

Technical concepts associated with BMD are presented to inform later analysis regarding the effectiveness of the U.S. missile defense program.

After their initial powered flight, ballistic missiles follow a trajectory that is determined only by the effects of gravity and atmospheric drag.[3] Ranges for the four classes of ballistic missiles are as follows:

- short-range ballistic missiles (SRBMs): 0 to 1,000 kilometers (km)
- medium-range ballistic missiles (MRBMs): 1,000 to 3,000 km

---

1. Raj Pattani is a graduate student in the Security Studies Program at Georgetown University's Edmund A. Walsh School of Foreign Service. In the summer of 2013, he worked as a research intern with the CSIS Project on Nuclear Issues. The views expressed here do not necessarily reflect those of CSIS or the Project on Nuclear Issues.

2. Portions of this essay draw on Colin H. Kahl, Raj Pattani, and Jacob Stokes, *If All Else Fails: The Challenges of Containing a Nuclear-Armed Iran* (Washington, DC: Center for a New American Security, 2013). The author wishes to thank Dr. Kahl for his comments on an earlier draft of this essay. Any errors in this essay are the sole responsibility of the author and the views expressed herein are the author's alone.

3. Joint Chiefs of Staff, *Countering Air and Missile Threats: Joint Publication 3-01* (Washington, DC: Joint Chiefs of Staff, March 2012), http://www.dtic.mil/doctrine/new_pubs/jp3_01.pdf; Ballistic Missile Defense Organization, *Ballistic Missile Defense Glossary* (Washington, DC: Department of Defense, June 1997), 26, http://www.defense.gov/specials/missiledefense/glossary.pdf.

- intermediate-range ballistic missiles (IRBMs): 3,000 to 5,500 km
- intercontinental ballistic missiles (ICBMs): more than 5,500 km[4]

SRBMs and MRBMs are considered theater ballistic missiles, while IRBMs and ICBMs are considered strategic ballistic missiles.[5]

Ballistic missiles can be solid-fueled or liquid-fueled. Solid-fueled rockets require less launch preparation and have shorter burn times than liquid-fuel analogues.[6] To illustrate, consider a notional ICBM launched from Iran, which would require approximately 40 minutes to reach a target in the United States. At the start of those 40 minutes, a solid-propellant ICBM would have 180 seconds of powered flight, while a liquid-propellant ICBM would require an additional 70 seconds to burn its fuel.[7]

There are four phases in the flight of a ballistic missile:[8]

1. *Boost phase:* The period of initial powered flight of the missile, where the "threat booster is still accelerating." A ballistic missile may use several rocket stages during its boost phase.[9]
2. *Midcourse ascent phase:* The period immediately following the end of powered flight, up to the point where the missile reaches its greatest height, called its "apogee."[10]
3. *Midcourse descent phase:* The period immediately following the apogee, through to the point where the missile re-enters the atmosphere.
4. *Terminal phase:* The period "as and after [the warhead re-enters] the atmosphere and becomes subject to drag and re-entry heating."[11]

Interception can occur during any of the four phases of missile flight, with each phase offering different opportunities and presenting different challenges for BMD systems:[12]

- Boost-phase intercept is appealing because it can eliminate a ballistic missile before countermeasures can be deployed; however, it is difficult because BMD systems would need to be close to the adversary's launch site and would need to detect, characterize, track, and engage the target in a very short period of time.

4. Kelsey Davenport, "Worldwide Ballistic Missile Inventories," Arms Control Association, January 2012, http://www.armscontrol.org/factsheets/missiles. Note that ranges for each class of missile vary by source; see Joint Chiefs of Staff, *Countering Air and Missile Threats*, for an alternative classification.

5. Davenport, "Worldwide Ballistic Missile Inventories."

6. Ibid.

7. National Research Council, *Making Sense of Ballistic Missile Defense: An Assessment of Concepts and Systems for U.S. Boost-Phase Missile Defense in Comparison to Other Alternatives* (Washington, DC: National Academies Press, 2012), 7–8.

8. Ibid., v. Sometimes the two midcourse phases are grouped together.

9. Ibid.

10. Ibid.

11. Ibid.

12. Ibid., 26.

- Midcourse intercept, during both ascent and descent, offers the longest time to engage the target and can allow a state to defend large areas with fewer interceptor launch sites; however, decoys and other countermeasures are released during the midcourse phase, making it difficult for BMD systems to identify the threatening missile. In order to overcome these challenges, some technologies focus on "ascent-phase intercept"—also called "early intercept"—to engage the target missile before countermeasures are deployed. Other BMD systems rely on effective midcourse discrimination to distinguish between the missile and its decoys.[13]

- Terminal intercept is useful because countermeasures generally become less effective during this final phase of flight. Drag forces affect the trajectory of decoys, because of their low weight, to a greater extent than they do the trajectory of reentry vehicles. This change in behavior in response to atmospheric drag makes it easier for BMD systems to discriminate between a threatening missile and innocuous decoys.[14] An important characteristic—and limitation—of terminal intercept BMD systems is that they generally defend more limited areas than systems based on boost and midcourse intercept.[15]

While decoys themselves make BMD a challenging endeavor, adversaries can also employ salvo launches, maneuver their missiles during midcourse flight, and attack BMD sensors in order to overcome defenses.[16] Even the lack of sophistication of an adversary's delivery vehicles can diminish the effectiveness of defenses: missiles that tumble end-over-end are more difficult targets to intercept.[17]

Iranian Ballistic Missile Capabilities

The effectiveness of any defensive system needs to be considered in the context of the particular threats it is designed to guard against. Key features of Iran's ballistic missile arsenal are described so later discussions can combine an understanding of technical BMD concepts with an understanding of Iran's ballistic missile capabilities.[18]

Iran's theater ballistic missiles can be used to restrict the U.S. military's "freedom of action" in the Middle East, while strategic ballistic missiles, if developed, would likely be

13. Ibid.

14. Ibid. In a hypothetical example, this reference explains that decoys, with their low mass, are "appreciably" affected by drag at altitudes as high as 100 km, where the air is still relatively thin; similar effects are seen on reentry vehicles only below altitudes of about 40 km.

15. Ibid., 80. This National Research Council report does not explicitly point out this limitation, but it discusses this characteristic when describing terminal high altitude air defense systems.

16. Ibid., 10, 102.

17. George N. Lewis and Theodore A. Postol, "How US strategic antimissile defense could be made to work," *Bulletin of the Atomic Scientists* 66, no. 6 (2010): 17–19.

18. While a discussion of threats would usually require an analysis of both capabilities and intent, this discussion will avoid passing judgment on complicated questions involving the aims of Iran and will instead focus on the more straightforward question of which capabilities Iran likely has at its disposal. Of course, also note that BMD systems are charged with protecting forces, partners, and the U.S. homeland from threats emerging from other states as well.

aimed at deterring U.S. influence in the region.[19] At the same time, both theater and strategic missiles can deter the United States—and Israel—from executing a preemptive or preventive strike against Iran; theater missiles would enable Iran to hold deployed U.S. forces and regional allies at risk, while strategic missiles would allow Iran to threaten European allies or the U.S. homeland.

As of December 2012 it appears that most of Iran's ballistic missile capabilities are the theater type, with analysts speculating about Iran's ability to develop longer-range strategic ballistic missiles in the near and medium terms.

Iran's known operational SRBM force includes the following three road-mobile systems, among others:

- Fateh-110, with a range of 200 km.
- Shahab-1, based on Soviet Scud B missiles obtained from North Korea, with a range of approximately 300 km.
- Shahab-2, based on Soviet Scud C missiles obtained from North Korea, with a range of approximately 500 km.[20]

It appears that all three systems can now be indigenously produced, although their precursors are based on missiles that appear to have been either procured externally or developed with support from foreign states or organizations outside Iran.[21]

Iran's SRBM arsenal also appears to include the Qiam ballistic missile, which may have a range of 500 to 1,000 km.[22] Details of Qiam are not well known, although some analysts point to it as evidence that Iran is capable of developing weapons systems with increasingly sophisticated guidance.[23]

Iran claims to have developed a new SRBM, named Khalij Fars, capable of targeting moving ships. This anti-ship ballistic missile has a reported range of 300 km, although some analysts say the missile does not likely have the precision required to threaten ships at such a long distance.[24]

---

19. Anthony H. Cordesman, Michael Gibbs, Bryan Gold, and Alexander Wilner, *Iran and the Gulf Military Balance—II: The Missile and Nuclear Dimensions: Working Draft* (Washington, DC: CSIS, November 2012), 3, http://csis.org/files/publication/Iran%20and%20Gulf%20Military%20Balance%20Part%20I%20-%2011-5-2012.pdf.

20. Steven A. Hildreth, *Iran's Ballistic Missile and Space Launch Programs* (Washington, DC: Congressional Research Service, December 2012), 18–19. The lists in this section are not exhaustive; they highlight the key weapons systems that have entered the discussion of Iran's ballistic missile capabilities. The Nuclear Threat Initiative (NTI) provides a detailed account of Iran's missiles; see Nuclear Threat Initiative, "Iran," November 2011, http://www.nti.org/country-profiles/iran/delivery-systems/.

21. Hildreth, *Iran's Ballistice Missile and Space Launch Programs*, 18; Cordesman et al., *Iran and the Gulf Military Balance—II*, 6–7.

22. Hildreth, *Iran's Ballistic Missile and Space Launch Programs*, 18.

23. Cordesman et al., *Iran and the Gulf Military Balance—II*, 29.

24. Ibid., 7.

Iran's known MRBM force includes the following systems:

- Shahab-3, with a range of 800 to 1,000 km. The Shahab-3 is notable because it is based on the North Korean No-dong 1 and can now likely be produced indigenously.[25] The Shahab-3 has been described as nuclear-capable.[26]
- Shahab-3M, also called Ghadr-1,[27] with a range between 1,000 and 2,000 km. The Shahab-3M might have been designed by North Korea; some analysts also speculate that Russian and Chinese experts assisted in modifications to the missile's nosecone.[28]
- Sejil, formerly named Ashura, with a range between 2,200 and 2,500 km.[29] The indigenously produced Sejil-2, tested in 2009, is significant because it is highly mobile and, being solid fueled, can launch with little preparation time. The missile is also thought to be easily concealed in mountainous terrain.[30] These characteristics could make Sejil an effective delivery system for nuclear warheads, should Iran choose to pursue such a capability.[31]

There have been reports that Iran acquired 18 Soviet R-27 submarine-launched MRBMs, which came in variants with ranges between 2,500 and 3,500 km.[32]

The possible development of Iranian strategic ballistic missiles has concerned the United States and its allies for some time. A December 2012 Congressional Research Service report is notable for its striking statement regarding the degree of urgency of the Iranian ICBM threat. A key paragraph from this document reads:

> Since the late 1990s, the U.S. intelligence community has repeatedly stated, with a number of caveats, that Iran would be able to test an ICBM capable of reaching the United States by 2015, which is at least 10,000 km away. Other countries do not necessarily share this assessment and Iran has long denied that it is developing an ICBM capable of reaching the United States. *Open-source analyses of ballistic missile tests in both Iran and North Korea raise questions about whether Iran may be developing a ballistic missile capable of reaching the United States or seeking to develop a space launch capability that could provide the technological basis for conversion to an ICBM.*[33]

---

25. Hildreth, *Iran's Ballistic Missile and Space Launch Programs*, 23.

26. Institute for Science and International Security (ISIS), "Iran in Brief: UN Report Cites 2 Unreported Long-Range Iranian Missile Launches," June 7, 2011, http://www.isisnucleariran.org/brief/detail/un-report-cites-2-unreported-long-range-iranian-missile-launches/.

27. Nuclear Threat Initiative, "Iran."

28. Hildreth, *Iran's Ballistic Missile and Space Launch Programs*, 23–24.

29. Ibid., 25.

30. David E. Sanger and Nazila Fathi, "Iran Test-Fires Missile With 1,200-Mile Range," *New York Times*, May 20, 2009, http://www.nytimes.com/2009/05/21/world/middleeast/21iran.html?_r=0. See Nuclear Threat Initiative, "Iran," for information on the indigenous development of this missile.

31. ISIS, "Iran in Brief."

32. Hildreth, *Iran's Ballistic Missile and Space Launch Programs*, 25–26.

33. Ibid., 35. Emphasis added. As this excerpt indicates, it is important to recognize that the Congressional Research Service report was based on unclassified sources.

The report explains that Iran does not appear to have received the technical support and advanced materials it would require from foreign partners in order to build an ICBM capable of reaching the United States. At the very least, the report "casts doubt" on earlier intelligence estimates that Iran could test an ICBM by 2015.[34] Sanctions also appear to be slowing Iranian ballistic missile development: while it has developed solid-fuel rockets indigenously, it relies on imports of key components and materials, such as aluminum powder, in the production of these rockets.[35]

Setting aside these doubts regarding Iran's ability to produce strategic ballistic missiles, developments in Iran's space program continue to raise fears about its ability to develop an ICBM in the near and medium terms. By some estimates, Iran's solid-fuel Safir rocket and liquid-fuel Simorgh could be used to develop an ICBM between 2015 and 2020. Even then, some believe that the testing Iran would require to convert its space technology into the type used for ballistic missiles "would provide the [United States] with sufficient warning to react."[36]

Current U.S. Ballistic Missile Defense Program

With the increasing sophistication of ballistic missiles being produced by outlier states, there is good reason for the United States to have pursued the development and deployment of BMD systems. The U.S. BMD program is described next.

Boost-phase BMD systems have been characterized as "currently not feasible."[37] Earlier attempts at developing boost-phase BMD systems have either been canceled or converted to technology development programs.[38]

The non-boost-phase BMD systems that comprise the core of the U.S. BMD program can be discussed in terms of the three missile defense missions: the defense of deployed forces, the defense of states friendly to the United States, and the defense of the U.S. homeland.[39]

BMD systems for the defense of deployed forces include the following:

1. *Aegis with Standard missile (SM) variants:* Sea-based Aegis BMD systems are currently deployed. They use SM-3 and SM-2 missiles for midcourse and terminal

34. Jim Wolf, "Iran's long-range missiles said to lag U.S. intelligence fears," Reuters, December 7, 2012, http://www.reuters.com/assets/print?aid=USBRE8B61C920121207.

35. Peter Crail, "Sanctions Seen Slowing Iran Nuclear Work," *Arms Control Today* (June 2011), http://www.armscontrol.org/act/2011_06/IranSanctions. This article includes quotes from Michael Elleman, a fellow at the International Institute for Strategic Studies, who explained that "forcing Iran to change suppliers frequently will stress their quality control system, and ultimately the reliability of [Iran's] solid propellant rockets and missiles."

36. Cordesman et al., *Iran and the Gulf Military Balance—II*, 22–23.

37. Defense Science Board, *Science and Technology Issues of Early Intercept Ballistic Missile Defense Feasibility* (Washington, DC: Defense Science Board, September 2011), 9, http://www.acq.osd.mil/dsb/reports/ADA552472.pdf.

38. National Research Council, *Making Sense of Ballistic Missile Defense*, 30–37.

39. The use of these three missions to organize a discussion of the BMD program follows National Research Council, *Making Sense of Ballistic Missile Defense*, 83–84.

intercept, respectively, of threatening SRBMs and MRBMs. Aegis systems previously only used ship-based sensors to autonomously complete interceptions. Recently, Aegis systems were given launch-on-remote (LOR) capability so that interceptors could be launched using inputs provided by sensors not located on the launching ship. Aegis systems are expected to receive engage-on-remote (EOR) capability in 2015 so that remote sensors can continue to communicate with interceptors after they are launched. In addition to BMD missions, Aegis is used in anti-aircraft warfare, anti-submarine warfare, and anti-surface warfare.[40] Aegis ships can protect territory from ballistic missiles hundreds of kilometers away.[41]

2. *Patriot Advanced Capability 3 (PAC-3):* PAC-3 uses radar and onboard sensors to perform terminal intercept of SRBMs and MRBMs. An improved PAC-3 missile is under development and should allow for greater intercept ranges.[42] PAC-3, while reliable, is used for relatively narrow "point defense" of U.S. forces and facilities.[43] Patriot systems have a range of approximately 100 km.[44]

3. *Terminal High Altitude Area Defense (THAAD):* THAAD can provide late midcourse and terminal intercept of SRBMs and MRBMs. THAAD is deployable on C-17 aircraft, making it useful for responding to regional threats as they arise.[45] In April 2013, for example, the Department of Defense announced that, in light of North Korean provocations earlier in the year, the United States would deploy a THAAD system to Guam.[46] THAAD has a range of 200 km and can engage missiles at an altitude of 150 km; its deployment is meant to reduce the number of missiles that would need to be intercepted by other systems, such as PAC-3, that provide nearer-range point defense of forces and facilities.[47]

In September 2009 the Obama administration announced its European Phased Adaptive Approach (PAA) to BMD. The PAA established milestones for developing and deploying increasingly sophisticated BMD systems over the course of about 11 years. The first three stages of the PAA are meant to protect states friendly to the United States. At present these

40. Ibid., 76–79.

41. Kahl et al., *If All Else Fails*, 37.

42. National Research Council, *Making Sense of Ballistic Missile Defense*, 81–83. Note that U.S. batteries frequently deploy older PAC-2 missiles alongside the newer PAC-3 missiles.

43. Anthony H. Cordesman and Khalid R. al-Rodhan, *Gulf Military Forces in an Era of Asymmetric Wars: Volume One* (Westport, CT: Praeger Security International/CSIS, 2007), 219–220.

44. "Patriot TMD," GlobalSecurity.org, January 8, 2013, http://www.globalsecurity.org/space/systems/patriot.htm.

45. National Research Council, *Making Sense of Ballistic Missile Defense*, 80–81.

46. "North Korea threats: US to move missile defences to Guam," BBC News, April 4, 2013, http://www.bbc.co.uk/news/world-us-canada-22021832. In a subsequent Department of Defense briefing, it appeared that THAAD had deployed to Guam by May 13, 2013. See "Department of Defense News Briefing with Lt. Gen. Wiercinski from the Pentagon," Department of Defense, May 13, 2013, http://www.defense.gov/transcripts/transcript.aspx?transcriptid=5237. For additional information about the Patriot and THAAD systems, see also "North Korea threats: Missile defenses in the region," BBC News, April 5, 2013, http://www.bbc.co.uk/news/world-asia-22028701.

47. "THAAD TMD," GlobalSecurity.org, June 6, 2013, http://www.globalsecurity.org/space/systems/thaad.htm.

phases are intended for the defense of southern Europe. The PAA structure has the following phases:[48]

1. *PAA Phase 1:* Deployed in 2011, PAA Phase 1 uses Aegis with sea-based SM-3 Block IA missiles and forward-based radar in order to intercept SRBMs and MRBMs targeting southern Europe. Each SM-3 Block IA interceptor is estimated to cost $9.6 million.
2. *PAA Phase 2:* Expected to be completed in 2015, PAA Phase 2 will use a more advanced SM-3 Block IB interceptor and one land-based Aegis site to provide greater coverage of southern Europe. Each SM-3 Block IB interceptor is estimated to cost $9.4 million.
3. *PAA Phase 3:* Expected to be completed in 2018, PAA Phase 3 will use a more advanced SM-3 Block IIA interceptor and an additional land-based Aegis site in order to extend BMD coverage to all North Atlantic Treaty Organization allies in Europe. Each SM-3 Block IIA interceptor is estimated to cost $15.7 million.

The administration of President George W. Bush invested in the development and deployment of a Ground-based Midcourse Defense (GMD) system to protect the U.S. homeland from ballistic missiles launched from outlier states such as North Korea and Iran.[49] The originally planned fourth phase of the PAA, subsequently canceled,[50] was meant to augment the existing GMD system in order to improve protection of the continental United States. Details are as follows:[51]

1. *GMD:* The GMD system is currently comprised of 26 ground-based interceptors (GBIs) at Fort Greely, Alaska and 4 GBIs at Vandenberg Air Force Base, California. Land-based radars in Alaska, California, Greenland, and the United Kingdom support the GMD system, along with sea-based radars on Aegis ships. Each GBI is estimated to cost $70 million.
2. *PAA Phase 4 (canceled in March 2013):* Originally expected to be completed in 2020, PAA Phase 4 was meant to use a more advanced SM-3 Block IIB missile in order to intercept a notional Iranian ICBM targeting the continental United States. Each SM-3 Block IIB interceptor was predicted to cost between $10 and $20 million.

In March 2013 Secretary of Defense Chuck Hagel announced that, in order to "stay ahead" of developments in North Korea and Iran, the Department of Defense would procure 14 additional GBIs for installation at Fort Greely, bringing the total number of GBIs in

48. Department of Defense, *Ballistic Missile Defense Review Report* (Washington, DC: Department of Defense, 2010), 24, http://www.defense.gov/bmdr/docs/BMDR%20as%20of%2026JAN10%200630_for%20web.pdf. Interceptor costs are from Defense Science Board, *Science and Technology Issues of Early Intercept Ballistic Missile Defense Feasibility*, 31.

49. Kahl et al., *If All Else Fails*, 34.

50. Tom Z. Collina, "The European Phased Adaptive Approach at a Glance," Arms Control Association, May 2013, http://www.armscontrol.org/factsheets/Phasedadaptiveapproach.

51. Department of Defense, *Ballistic Missile Defense Review Report*, 15, 24. Interceptor costs are from Defense Science Board, *Science and Technology Issues of Early Intercept Ballistic Missile Defense Feasibility*, 31.

the United States arsenal to 44 by the year 2017.[52] At the same time, it appears that the Department of Defense canceled deployments under PAA Phase 4. Even though PAA Phase 4 *deployments* are canceled, the SM-3 Block IIB program itself appears to have only been downgraded to a technology development program.[53]

Survey of Critiques of the Ballistic Missile Defense Program

By combining a technical understanding of basic BMD concepts, an appreciation for the Iranian ballistic missile threat, and knowledge regarding the U.S. BMD program, it becomes possible to explore critiques of ballistic missile defense. It is acknowledged that there are strategic implications of BMD that are important for national security strategy, in particular with regard to the U.S.-Russian and U.S.-Chinese relationships. This discussion sets aside these issues and focuses instead on the ability of the U.S. BMD program to execute its mission.

The BMD program appears to be well suited for the defense of deployed forces, might have some areas of concern for the regional defense of states friendly to the United States, and provokes the most controversy over its effectiveness in defending the continental United States.

DEFENSE OF DEPLOYED FORCES

In its detailed study of the U.S. BMD program, the National Research Council writes that the Aegis system with LOR and EOR capability, PAC-3, and THAAD "will [together] provide, where appropriate, adequate coverage for defense of U.S. and allied deployed forces."[54] Concerns regarding the ability of the United States to field BMD equipment to defend deployed forces do not appear to be centered on the effectiveness of the anti-missile systems themselves. One critic suggests that the United States needs to procure and field more of these theater BMD systems to defend against a large Iranian arsenal of SRBMs and MRBMs.[55]

REGIONAL DEFENSE

Reviews of the BMD program's ability to provide regional defense for countries friendly to the United States are less positive, although the expert reports produced by the National Research Council and the Defense Science Board are mostly encouraging. The National

52. Amaani Lyle, "Hagel: U.S. Bolstering Missile Defense," American Forces Press Service, March 15, 2013, http://www.defense.gov/news/newsarticle.aspx?id=119543.

53. Tom Z. Collina, "Pentagon Shifts Gears on Missile Defense," *Arms Control Today* (April 2013), http://www.armscontrol.org/act/2013_04/Pentagon-Shifts-Gears-on-Missile-Defense.

54. National Research Council, *Making Sense of Ballistic Missile Defense*, 105.

55. Eddie Boxx, "Countering the Iranian Missile Threat in the Middle East," Washington Institute for Near East Policy, October 18, 2012, http://www.washingtoninstitute.org/policy-analysis/view/countering-the-iranian-missile-threat-in-the-middle-east.

Research Council writes that, with EOR, the "first three phases of the European Phased Adaptive Approach . . . are expected to provide defense for Europe against a limited ballistic missile attack for deployed U.S. and allied forces within the region and the Middle East."[56] Similarly, the Defense Science Board writes that "the basic components in inventory now, namely Aegis ships with radars and long-range interceptor missiles, are well suited as the foundation of the regional defense mission, including the defense of Europe," and goes on to say that, setting aside some concerns about early intercept, the "feasibility of achieving the basic objectives of the PAA has been well established by the current and planned Missile Defense Agency program—no fundamental roadblocks or major technical barriers to success" are apparent.[57] Critics have expressed concern regarding the SM-3, with the National Research Council stating that the SM-3 Block IIA has "fallen far short of its originally planned performance."[58] One pair of experts suggest the SM-3 has a success rate as low as 10 percent in recent evaluations, saying the interceptors have not decisively destroyed target warheads during testing,[59] although the Missile Defense Agency disputes this.[60]

CONTINENTAL DEFENSE

The greatest concerns exist regarding the defense of the continental United States. The National Research Council states that the GMD system is "limited in its ability to perform the US homeland defense mission," citing concerns in midcourse discrimination and cost. It also suggests that the eastern United States is "poorly protected by the current GMD system." In addition to the establishment of a new interceptor launch site on the east coast (a proposition apparently of interest to Congress), it advocates for an evolved GMD system, called GMD-E, which would have a more effective kill vehicle and improved midcourse discrimination.[61] The Missile Defense Agency characterized some of these criticisms as routine in its initial response to the National Research Council report. One expert outside the Department of Defense questioned the technical feasibility of the GMD-E system.[62]

Some academics criticize the Department of Defense for claiming that the continental United States is protected from ICBMs with existing systems, saying that such claims are

56. National Research Council, *Making Sense of Ballistic Missile Defense*, 106.

57. Defense Science Board, *Science and Technology Issues of Early Intercept Ballistic Missile Defense Feasibility*, 8, 23.

58. National Research Council, *Making Sense of Ballistic Missile Defense*, 90.

59. George N. Lewis and Theodore A. Postol, "A Flawed and Dangerous U.S. Missile Defense Plan," *Arms Control Today* (May 2010), http://www.armscontrol.org/act/2010_05/Lewis-Postol.

60. William J. Broad and David E. Sanger, "Review Cites Flaws in U.S. Antimissile Program," *New York Times*, May 17, 2010, http://www.nytimes.com/2010/05/18/world/18missile.html.

61. National Research Council, *Making Sense of Ballistic Missile Defense*, 86, 104, 130; and Greg Thielmann, "Threat Assessment Brief: Iran's Missile Program and Its Implications for U.S. Missile Defense," Arms Control Association, January 30, 2013, 3, http://www.armscontrol.org/threats/Irans-Missile-Program-and-Its-Implications-for-US-Missile-Defense. Thielmann notes that, in the National Defense Authorization Act, Congress asked the Department of Defense to study options for basing additional interceptors on the east coast of the United States.

62. William J. Broad, "U.S. Missile Defense Strategy is Flawed, Expert Panel Finds," *New York Times*, September 11, 2012, http://www.nytimes.com/2012/09/12/science/us-missile-defense-protections-are-called-vulnerable.html.

"fantastical, audacious, and dangerous."[63] They argue that existing interceptors are not effective, citing difficulties in identifying the location of warheads inside an incoming missile, particularly when the threatening missile may tumble end-over-end. They also question the degree of realism in Department of Defense tests of missile defense systems. In light of their concerns regarding the U.S. BMD program, these academics advocate for a missile defense system based on unmanned aerial vehicles.[64] This drone-based system appears questionable, though; it would be difficult to bring drones into contested areas and the success of the system would depend on adversaries using known, fixed launch sites.

Recommendations

The preceding analysis suggests some ways in which the U.S. BMD program can be made more effective.

The United States should take advantage of the reduced speed with which the Iranian ballistic missile program appears to have evolved in recent years. In terms of qualitative capabilities, it appears that the current U.S. BMD program is able to defend against the most pressing existing Iranian missiles, which, at present, are mainly of the theater type. There will always be concerns regarding the small number of U.S. interceptors available to counter the larger number of ballistic missiles in the Iranian arsenal. To manage these concerns, the Obama administration should continue to procure and deploy proven technologies for theater ballistic missile defense in a way that is commensurate with the threat assessments of the intelligence community. A judgment regarding the quantity and type of SM-3, PAC-3, or THAAD interceptors that should be deployed in the near term is outside the scope of the current discussion.

At the same time, while theater BMD systems appear effective in protecting deployed U.S. forces and critical facilities, they do not provide full coverage for the territory of U.S. partners in the Middle East. As such, it will be important for these U.S. partners, particularly the United Arab Emirates and Saudi Arabia, to continually upgrade and integrate their BMD systems and supporting sensors.[65]

Given doubts over whether Iran is actually pursuing an ICBM, the United States has time to develop effective strategic BMD systems without employing a costly strategy that concurrently develops and deploys technologies. As such, unless the threat from adversaries evolves, as happened with North Korea in March 2013, the United States should not make significant investments in operationalizing new BMD systems for ICBMs until clear technical goals have been met, especially with regard to midcourse discrimination.[66] This

63. Lewis and Postal, "How US strategic antimissile defense could be made to work," 9.

64. Ibid., 9–12, 16–17.

65. Kahl et al., *If All Else Fails*, 40–41.

66. While this discussion does not seek to make technical recommendations, it is worth noting that the expert panels of the National Research Council and Defense Science Board both advocated for technology development to facilitate "shoot-assess-shoot" firing doctrines, improved sensor integration, and better midcourse discrimination. These appear to be straightforward suggestions, although it is recognized that some

is in line with an April 2012 Government Accountability Office report that recommended reducing concurrency in the Missile Defense Agency's development and acquisition processes.[67]

At the same time, if intelligence estimates shift or it otherwise becomes clear that Iran is developing nuclear weapons, the United States should consider purchasing additional GMD interceptors—provided they meet the Department of Defense's technical requirements—as it did in March 2013 in response to North Korean provocations. Further, if Iran develops nuclear weapons, the United States should begin construction of an east coast GMD interceptor launch site.[68]

BMD has an important role in the national security architecture of the United States. Wise investments today will help ensure the United States fields systems that can meet tomorrow's threats.

---

goals, particularly those involving midcourse discrimination, will continue to challenge scientists and engineers.

67. U.S. Government Accountability Office (GAO), *Missile Defense: Opportunity Exists to Strengthen Acquisitions by Reducing Concurrency*, GAO-12-486 (Washington, DC: GAO, April 2012), 27–28, http://www.gao.gov/assets/600/590277.pdf. For one of the recommendations in this report, GAO references Department of Defense concerns about balancing the need to reduce concurrency with a need to maintain the industrial base for missile defense (see page 31).

68. Kahl et al., *If All Else Fails*, 35.

Defining the Costs of the U.S. Nuclear Weapons Complex: Reconstructing the 1251 Report

Marc Quint[1]

To meet a diverse array of threats, the United States maintains a strategic triad of nuclear-armed heavy bombers, ballistic missile submarines, and land-based intercontinental ballistic missiles, as well as a small stockpile of tactical nuclear weapons for delivery by combat aircraft. Most of these systems date to the late 1970s and early 1980s, meaning they will reach the end of their lifecycles around the same time in the 2030s. The long lead times required to recapitalize all three legs of the triad necessitate initial funding now and will stretch over the next quarter century. Careful planning is essential to avoid cost growth and schedule delays that could impose reductions beyond those the United States might choose to make based on national security grounds alone. Unfortunately, the current nuclear weapons funding blueprint is the 1251 Report—a 10-year projection that accounts for only 10 percent of the total costs to recapitalize the triad. A careful reconstruction reveals that the 1251 Report omits significant costs, particularly beyond the arbitrary 10-year time horizon, that policymakers must begin planning for immediately. Refusing to reassess current plans may threaten the long-term viability of the U.S. nuclear deterrent.

Impetus of the 1251 Report

With the sudden imposition of fiscal austerity in the United States, many independent groups have attempted to estimate the amount of money spent on nuclear weapons. The proliferation of outside estimates reflects the absence of a single, authoritative estimate of spending. The existing budgetary construct for strategic forces, Major Force Program 1 (MFP-1), is inadequate due to its inclusion of both nuclear and conventional programs, while excluding some nuclear deterrence categories. The Secretary of Defense Task Force noted the need for the Department of Defense (DOD) to establish "a new capability portfolio comprising all program elements directly related to nuclear deterrence, whether currently

1. Marc Quint is a graduate research assistant at the James Martin Center for Nonproliferation Studies. This project has only been possible with the continued guidance and support of Jon Wolfsthal and Jeffrey Lewis.

categorized in Major Force Program-1 . . . or elsewhere in the defense program and budget structure."[2]

As part of the Senate's advice and consent for ratification of the New Strategic Arms Reduction Treaty, Section 1251 of the National Defense Authorization Act of 2010 required the president to provide Congress with a report detailing nuclear weapons spending over the next 10 years (fiscal years [FY] 2011 through 2020).[3] The subsections of Section 1251 related to delivery systems state that the report shall include:

> (C) A description of the plan to maintain delivery platforms for nuclear weapons.
>
> (D) An estimate of budget requirements, including the costs associated with the plans . . . over a 10-year period.

The Obama administration submitted the 1251 Report in May 2010, followed by an amended version in November. The reports are classified, but the White House submitted an unclassified summary of the 1251 Report as Amended to Congress (hereafter, references to the 1251 Report refer to the unclassified fact sheet describing the November 2010 version as amended).[4] Senior administration officials have also provided unclassified testimony regarding the administration's modernization plans and the 1251 Report.[5]

The 1251 Report detailed nuclear weapons spending of approximately $214 billion over FY 2011–2020: about $88 billion for nuclear weapons activities at the Department of Energy (DOE) and approximately $125 billion for the DOD to sustain and modernize the triad. Much of the debate about whether the 1251 Report fully captured the cost of the U.S. nuclear enterprise centers on the $125 billion estimate for the DOD. The 1251 Report does not provide a detailed breakdown of the spending, although it does provide figures for some of the most important modernization programs *over 10 years*:

- $29.4 billion for the *Ohio*-class submarine replacement, the SSBN(X)
- $1.7 billion for the Long-Range Strike-Bomber (LRS-B)
- $1 billion for a new intercontinental ballistic missile (ICBM) and Long-Range Stand-Off (LRSO) cruise missile

2. James R. Schlesinger et al., *Report of the Secretary of Defense Task Force on DoD Nuclear Weapons Management: Phase II: Review of the DoD Nuclear Mission* (Arlington, VA: Secretary of Defense Task Force on DoD Nuclear Weapons Management, December 2008), vii, http://www.defense.gov/npr/docs/DOD%20NW%20Management%20Phase%20II%20Schlesinger.pdf.

3. National Defense Authorization Act for Fiscal Year 2010, Public Law No. 111-84, § 1251 *U.S. Statutes at Large* 123 (2009): 2190, http://www.gpo.gov/fdsys/pkg/STATUTE-123/pdf/STATUTE-123-Pg2190.pdf.

4. November 2010 Update to the National Defense Authorization Act of FY 2010 Section 1251 Report, http://nucleardiner.com/blogs/wp-content/uploads/2011/10/1251-1.pdf.

5. House Committee on Armed Services, *Statement of General C.R. Kehler, Commander, U.S. Strategic Command, Before the House Committee on Armed Services*, 113th Congress, 1st session, March 5, 2013, 1–19, http://www.stratcom.mil/files/2013-03-05-posture.pdf; Senate Committee on Armed Services, *The New START and the Implications for National Security*, 111th Congress, 2nd session, July 20, 2010, 192–198, http://www.gpo.gov/fdsys/pkg/CHRG-111shrg65071/pdf/CHRG-111shrg65071.pdf.

Overall, the narrative text of the 1251 Report details only about $32 billion of $125 billion slated for the DOD—roughly 25 percent. Understanding the strengths and weaknesses of the 1251 Report requires a better understanding of the remaining 75 percent.

Reconstructing the 1251 Report

It is possible to complete an approximate reconstruction of the 1251 Report based on budget documents prepared by the DOD and the armed services, when combined with congressional testimony and other unclassified information. It is important to note that procurement of the first SSBN(X) has been delayed to FY 2021, thereby pushing it beyond the scope of the 1251 Report and reducing the projected costs in this time frame. However, the increase in funding for the LRS-B nearly mirrors the reduction in SSBN(X) funding, keeping the overall $125 billion estimate roughly the same.

Table 1 shows an approximate reconstruction of the 1251 Report by service (Navy and Air Force) and account (procurement; research, development, testing, and evaluation [RDT&E]; operations and maintenance; and military personnel). Since the 1251 Report specifies the 10-year costs as estimated by the DOD, and budget documents at best provide data through FY 2018, the remaining out-year spending is listed as a remainder.

The reconstruction is able to account for approximately $115 billion of a projected $125 billion over 10 years—about 92 percent of spending. Possible explanations for this discrepancy will be discussed later.

Table 1 Reconstructed 1251 Report by Service (billion $ approximation)

FY 2011–2020	*Navy*	*Air Force*	*Total*
Procurement	16.1	2.2	18.3
Research and development	11.1	8.4	19.5
Operations and maintenance	12.1	22.3	34.4
Military personnel	2.9	18.0	20.9
SSBN(X) remainder	19.6	0	19.6
LRS-B remainder	0	1.7	1.7
LRSO remainder	0	0.8	0.8
ICBM remainder	0	*	*
Subtotals	61.8	53.4	115.2
1251 Report			~125

* The 1251 Report contained only $20 million to begin work on an analysis of alternatives for a new ICBM.

Table 2 Fiscal Years 2011–2018 RDT&E Budget for Long-Range Strike Bomber, Long-Range Stand-Off Cruise Missile, and B-2 and B-52 Systems (million $)

	2011	*2012*	*2013*	*2014*	*2015*	*2016*	*2017*	*2018*
Long range strike bomber	192.816	289.573	291.742	379.437	1,045.328	1,818.046	2,707.315	2,836.047
Long-range stand-off cruise missile		9.926	2.004	5	40.5	203.6	349.3	440.3
B-2 defensive management system			281.056	303.5	259.4	168.3	115	89.7
B-2 modernization	244.732	21.751	21.759	85.858	112.681	45.932	12.636	18.04
B2 and B-52 baseline support		9.523	7.875	14.336	15.916	13.81	14.045	14.298
B2 and B-52 EHF Satcom and computer		123.987	6.336					
B2 and B-52 defensive management system		46.427						

Note: RDT&E—research, development, test, and evaluation; EHF Satcom—extremely high-frequency satellite communications.

The method for approximating the 1251 Report is rather straightforward. Unclassified budget data is available for FY 2011–2018, as stated in the FY 2013 and FY 2014 documents.[6] Table 2 shows the extrapolated FY 2011–2018 RDT&E budget breakdown for the LRS-B, LRSO cruise missile, and B-2 and B-52 systems.

The projections in Table 2 are explicit for procurement and research and development (R&D), but not for operations and maintenance (O&M) or military personnel (MILPERS). To determine procurement and R&D costs for FY 2019–2020, the spending for FY 2014–2018 (the five years of the Future Years Defense Program) is averaged and flat-lined across the final two years. This is admittedly imperfect but provides a reasonable approximation of expected costs. The remainder of the projected costs of the SSBN(X) from the 1251 Report ($19.6 billion) are then added to the end because it is unclear how those funds will be spread over the final two years. However, it is known that the 1251 Report assumed procurement of the first submarine in FY 2019.[7]

The projections for O&M and MILPERS are more difficult to estimate. Unclassified budget documents provide data for only three years: previous (FY 2012), current (FY 2013), and future (FY 2014). To extrapolate data for years FY 2015–2017, deflators are provided for

6. "Fiscal Year 2014 Air Force Budget Materials," Air Force Financial Management and Comptroller, http://www.saffm.hq.af.mil/budget/; "Fiscal Year 2014 Department of the Navy Budget Materials," Office of the Assistant Secretary of the Navy–Financial Management and Comptroller, http://www.finance.hq.navy.mil/fmb/14pres/BOOKS.htm.

7. November 2010 Update to the Section 1251 Report.

Table 3 Comparison of Fiscal Year 2013 Budget for Air Force Nuclear Deterrent Operations and the Reconstructed 1251 Report (million $)

	Air Force Budget	*Reconstructed 1251 Report*	*Discrepancy*
Procurement	330	235	−95
Research and development	810	1,080	271
Totals	1,140	1,315	

both categories (O&M and MILPERS) in the DOD Green Book for FY 2013.[8] Since deflators are not provided for FY 2018–2020, the projections are averaged for FY 2013–2017 and flat-lined across the final three years.

Navy O&M costs are clearly defined under the Fleet Ballistic Missile Operations category,[9] while MILPERS is not. A Navy Visibility and Management of Operation and Support Costs (VAMOSC) report on the *Ohio*-class ballistic missile submarine (SSBN) for fiscal years 1992–1996 shows an average of $286.7 million per year for personnel costs when converted to FY 2013 dollars.[10] This average alone is used to extrapolate for all other years because current VAMOSC data is treated as official-use-only.[11]

Air Force O&M and MILPERS costs are more ambiguous. Within the FY 2013 budget overview the Air Force provided a graph entitled "Nuclear Deterrent Operations" that showed a $5.1 billion total and a rough outline of O&M, MILPERS, military construction, R&D, and procurement.[12] Using boxes to overlay the chart, the proportions of each category compared to the $5.1 billion total equals roughly $1.8 billion and $2.2 billion per year for MILPERS and O&M costs, respectively. O&M- and MILPERS-specific deflators were then used to extrapolate for other years.

The Air Force chart can also be used to double-check the procurement and R&D estimates outlined in Table 2. Table 3 provides a comparison of the Air Force's FY 2013 budget for nuclear deterrent operations and the reconstructed 1251 Report.

Combining R&D and procurement, the measurements suggest about $1.140 billion, while budget data totals $1.315 billion. It is difficult to determine the cause of these discrepancies. Some of the overall discrepancy appears to result from funding in FY 2018 to

8. Office of the Under Secretary of Defense, *National Defense Budget Estimates for FY 2013* (Washington, DC: Department of Defense, March 2012), http://comptroller.defense.gov/defbudget/fy2013/FY13_Green_Book.pdf.
9. Office of the Assistant Secretary of the Navy–Financial Management and Comptroller, *Department of the Navy Fiscal Year (FY) 2013 Budget Estimates* (Washington, DC: Department of the Navy, 2012), 237, http://www.finance.hq.navy.mil/fmb/13pres/OMN_Vol1_book.pdf.
10. Federation of American Scientists, "SSBN-726CL," http://www.fas.org/man//dod-101/sys/ship/docs/ssbn-726cl.htm.
11. Michael Carey, Naval Center for Cost Analysis, e-mail message to author, March 20, 2013.
12. U.S. Air Force, *United States Air Force FY 2013 Budget Overview* (Washington, DC: Department of Defense, February 2012), 34, http://www.saffm.hq.af.mil/shared/media/document/AFD-120209-052.pdf.

2020 when estimates are least clear. The Air Force and Navy may also partially allocate funds for systems that have dual conventional and strategic missions. Overall, however, the approximation shows good agreement and is sufficient to illustrate the strengths and weaknesses of the process laid out in Section 1251 of the National Defense Authorization Act.

Exclusions from the Budget

Although the reconstruction of the 1251 Report is approximate, the findings are close enough to identify costs that are excluded and may be of interest to policymakers:

- The 10-year timeframe appears too arbitrary given that the administration is committing now to programs that will entail significant costs just past that time horizon. This is especially true for the SSBN(X) program. The 1251 Report counts $29.4 billion for the SSBN(X) over 10 years, but the total cost of the program is likely to be between $100 and 110 billion.[13] A better approach would be to make full lifecycle cost estimates for recapitalizing each leg of the triad. This has not been done in a systematic way since a series of Government Accountability Office studies in the early 1990s.[14]
- The 1251 Report treats costs that are difficult to estimate as zero. The LRS-B, for example, had not progressed past its early research and development stages. As a result, the Air Force could estimate only $1.7 billion in spending. In the most recent budget, the Air Force now estimates the costs for the LRS-B to be $9.6 billion through 2018. The Air Force ultimately plans to procure 80 to 100 aircraft at a total cost between $44 and 55 billion.[15] The projections for a new ICBM and LRSO were also far too low. An $800 million estimate for the LRSO now stands at $1.1 billion through 2018 and will increase in the 2020s. The 1251 Report contains essentially no funding (only $20 million) for a new ICBM. Finally, command and control funding is entirely absent, yet is in need of modernization.

Implications for Defense Procurement

The 1251 Report provides some insight into funding for the recapitalization of the nuclear triad, but omits programs that may threaten the sustainability of strategic forces. Overall, the 1251 Report accounts for only 10 percent of the full cost to replace the existing delivery

---

13. Congressional Budget Office (CBO), *An Analysis of the Navy's Fiscal Year 2013 Shipbuilding Plan* (Washington, DC: CBO, July 2012), 19, http://www.cbo.gov/sites/default/files/cbofiles/attachments/07-25-12-NavyShipbuilding_0.pdf.

14. See Government Accountability Office (GAO), *ICBM Modernization: Small ICBM Weapon System Status and Current Issues* (Washington, DC: GAO, September 1991), http://www.gao.gov/products/NSIAD-91-275; GAO, *B-2 Bomber: Acquisition Cost Estimates* (Washington, DC: GAO, February 1993), http://www.gao.gov/products/NSIAD-93-48BR.

15. Department of Defense, *Annual Aviation Inventory and Funding Plan, Fiscal Years 2012–2041* (Washington, DC: Department of Defense, 2011), 22, http://www.airforcemag.com/SiteCollectionDocuments/Reports/2011/May%202011/Day25/AircraftProctPlan2012-2041_052511.pdf.

systems at today's levels—only $32 billion of an expected $300–400 billion over a 30-year period. Funding levels appear manageable over the life of the 1251 Report, but over the time horizon expenditures increase dramatically. Looking at planned procurement schedules and end of lifecycle data, the period between 2025 and 2030 may become a procurement chokepoint when the DOD must attempt to pay to replace one-third to one-half of the force in five to six years—all while procuring major conventional systems such as the Joint Strike Fighter. If the LRS-B and ICBM programs do not end by 2030, it is possible that the chokepoint could stretch into the 2030s.

Competition for funding with other priorities, including conventional forces, may result in a feedback loop of cost growth and schedule delays. The ultimate result could be deeper reductions than might otherwise be made with a more comprehensive planning process. Complaints from the Navy that funding for the SSBN(X) will hinder the overall shipbuilding effort, causing major reductions in the overall force, partly reflect service prerogatives, but they are not without merit.[16] Moreover, it is not out of the question to imagine similar challenges if the Air Force attempts a simultaneous replacement of bombers and ICBMs. While the SSBN(X) schedule is relatively inflexible due to the decommissioning process of the current *Ohio*-class submarine beginning in 2027, it is less clear that current bombers and ICBMs need to be replaced in the near future. The service lives of the B-2 and B-52 will last beyond 2040,[17] and the Air Force is investigating options to extend the life of the Minuteman-III ICBM beyond 2030.[18]

Careful planning now could allow the United States to manage a process of future reductions consistent with national security requirements. The alternative is an uncertain process in which the United States may spend more to procure far fewer and less capable systems. As a first step, Congress and the Obama administration could consider complementing the 1251 Report with an estimate of the full lifecycle costs to recapitalize the U.S. nuclear deterrent. Such a process would allow the DOD to identify risks in modernizing U.S. strategic forces and develop approaches to mitigate those risks.

16. Walter Pincus, "Budget Cuts Could Reshape the Country's Ship Supply, Official Says," *Washington Post*, May 1, 2013, http://articles.washingtonpost.com/2013-05-01/world/38955629_1_ssbns-warheads-triad.

17. House Committee on Armed Services, *Statement of General C. R. Kehler*, 13.

18. Ibid.; Federal Business Opportunities, "Broad Agency Announcement—Ground-Based Strategic Deterrence," BAA-AFNWC-XZ-13-001Rev2, March 29, 2013, https://www.fbo.gov/spg/USAF/AFMC/377CONSKOC/BAA-AFNWC-XZ-13-001/listing.html.

Maintaining Nuclear Deterrence and Stability: Why the Status Quo of Nuclear Alert Rates Is Effective and Should Remain

Angela Weaver[1]

In the current nuclear atmosphere, stability is the greatest safety net. Maintaining a portion of U.S. nuclear forces on alert is one of the best means of maintaining stable deterrence both day-to-day and in crisis. There are currently 450 Minuteman III intercontinental ballistic missiles (ICBMs) on day-to-day alert in addition to "a small number" (about 40 percent) of the submarine-launched ballistic missiles (SLBMs) aboard the 14 *Ohio*-class submarines (each of which can carry up to 24 SLBMs).[2] ICBMs on alert are equipped with a nuclear warhead and have their "solid-fuel engines powered up" but are not targeted at any specific sites; they remain on "broad ocean area targeting."[3] The SLBMs are also equipped with nuclear warheads, four to five each on average.[4] Each of these nuclear forces is on alert and available for launch on presidential directive. The entire strategic bomber leg of the nuclear triad was removed from alert in 1991.[5]

However, a debate over whether to further de-alert some or all of the U.S. nuclear arsenal continues. Proponents of the idea claim that maintaining the current alert posture perpetuates a Cold War relationship with Russia and a reliance on an outdated force structure and nuclear strategy. They argue that the threat of nuclear terrorism and the risk of accidental or unauthorized use is too high to justify keeping these weapons on alert.

---

1. Angela Weaver is a recent graduate of Wake Forest University. In the summer and fall of 2013 she worked as a research intern for the Project on Nuclear Issues. The views expressed here are her own and do not necessarily reflect those of the Center for Strategic and International Studies or the Project on Nuclear Issues.
2. U.S. Navy, "Fact File: Fleet Ballistic Missile Submarines—SSBN," November 27, 2012, http://www.navy.mil/navydata/fact_display.asp?cid=4100&tid=200&ct=4.
3. Walter Pincus, "ICBM Crew's Work Largely Unchanged Since the Cold War," *Washington Post*, November 23, 2007, http://www.washingtonpost.com/wp-dyn/content/article/2007/11/22/AR2007112201294.html.
4. Hans M. Kristensen and Matthew McKinzie, *Reducing Alert Rates of Nuclear Weapons* (Geneva: UN Institute for Disarmament Research, 2012), 1.
5. Wade Boese, "Nuclear Weapons Alert Status Debated," *Arms Control Today* (December 2007), http://www.armscontrol.org/act/2007_12/NuclearAlert.

Although today's world is different than that of the Cold War, and the role of nuclear weapons in U.S. national security strategy has been reduced, the value of nuclear weapons remains high. As Keir Lieber and Darryl Press write, "All that has changed are the seats at the table."[6] As more states acquire nuclear weapons and nuclear relationships become more complicated and multilateral, an effective nuclear deterrent will remain an important aspect of defense. The current alert rates of U.S. nuclear weapons keep the U.S. deterrent credible day-to-day and prevent the rapid escalation of crisis situations into violent misunderstandings and nuclear conflict, no matter the adversary.

The Stability of the Alert Status Quo

Although many debates surround nuclear weapons, the fact remains that deterrence provides a compelling explanation for the absence of major power wars between nuclear states. Maintaining a portion of our nuclear weapons on alert remains a key component of a successful U.S. deterrent strategy. Opponents of the policy often describe the alert status as "hair trigger," but the validity of that statement has been contested vigorously by those who operate those forces. United States Strategic Command has stated that classifying the alert status as "hair trigger" is incorrect and "ignores the safeguards, deliberate actions, and procedures required in order to employ nuclear weapons."[7] They suggest the term "day-to-day" as a more accurate representation of the alert status, meaning "U.S. policy is not to rely on a 'launch on warning' strategy" but one in which "under any credible scenario, a sufficient number of nuclear weapons would survive to respond" to a nuclear attack by an aggressor.[8]

The day-to-day status allows for greater flexibility and varying degrees of response to different situations and tensions. Proponents of de-alert argue that maintaining ICBMs on alert creates a greater risk for a "use or lose" situation to occur.[9] However, maintaining the alert status of some ICBMs strengthens deterrence—in that adversaries view a first strike as less likely to succeed—and therefore reduces the temptation to attempt to force the United States into a "use or lose" situation.

The U.S. relationship with Russia has improved dramatically since the end of the Cold War, but it is not yet ready for de-alert. Misunderstandings still often occur, especially arising from foreign policy decisions. The U.S. reaction to Russia's support for the Assad regime in Syria and the Russian reaction to U.S. plans to build ballistic missile defenses in Poland and the Czech Republic serve as examples of an evolving relationship that is still

6. Keir A. Lieber and Daryl G. Press, *Coercive Nuclear Campaigns in the 21st Century: Understanding Adversary Incentives and Options for Nuclear Escalation* (Monterey, CA: Naval Postgraduate School Center on Contemporary Conflict, March 2013), 8, http://www.hsdl.org/?view&did=734062.

7. Arms Control Association, "Text of Nov. 28 E-mail from Strategic Command responding to ACT's questions on the alert status of U.S. nuclear weapons," November 2007, http://www.armscontrol.org/interviews/20071204_STRATCOM.

8. Ibid.

9. Ibid. "Use or lose" refers to a situation where the United States would have to launch its nuclear arsenal or risk the possibility that any unused weapons would be destroyed in an adversary's counterforce strike.

often characterized by high tensions and the possibility for friction.[10] In such an atmosphere, the security and stability of the nuclear deterrent are invaluable as the two nations work to create a more positive relationship.

Bruce Blair, cofounder of Global Zero and president of the World Security Institute, has long written about the need to de-alert. His argument centers on two concerns: (1) the idea that reliance on nuclear weapons is excessive and legitimizes the proliferation of nuclear weapons by nonnuclear states and (2) the worry that the continued aging of Russian and U.S. nuclear forces makes accidental or unauthorized launch more likely and dangerous.[11] He shares a popular view that nuclear weapons play a dangerously central role in the U.S. relationship with Russia. By de-alerting, the argument goes, the relationship could then pivot away from nuclear terms, setting a precedent that nuclear weapons are not a priority in national security strategy. While this is an important goal, the situation and the relationship are too complicated to accommodate such a simple solution. As long as Moscow continues to see its nuclear arsenal as the primary reason Russia remains a major power,[12] and as long as the U.S.-Russia relationship retains the potential for armed conflict, nuclear weapons will remain a central element of U.S.-Russian relations.

If the United States and Russia were to fully de-alert their nuclear arsenals, the pressure to re-alert in a crisis situation would be intense and, if attempted, would dramatically exacerbate the crisis, making conflict a more likely outcome. Dramatic escalation of this nature has happened before in the history of relations between major powers.

The outbreak of World War I in August 1914 serves as an example of a political-military situation in which tense alliance relationships caused a military buildup that could only succeed under large-scale, rapid mobilization. A situation such as this creates the "presence of threats to the security of both sides," a scenario that "can turn the dispute into a zero-sum game."[13] While the U.S. relationship with Russia has progressed, each power can still perceive the other as a potential adversary, so the potential for political conflict continues to exist. If political disagreements lead to a crisis situation, the current alert posture would stabilize what could otherwise result in a hostile zero-sum scenario and a race to re-alert.

10. Amy F. Woolf, "Nuclear Force Posture and Alert Rates: Issues and Options" (paper presented at the seminar on "Re-framing De-Alert: Decreasing the Operational Readiness of Nuclear Weapons Systems in the U.S.-Russia Context," Yverdon, Switzerland, June 21–23, 2009), 7–9, http://www.ewi.info/system/files/Woolf.pdf.

11. Michael Krepon, "De-Alerting and De-Legitimization," *Arms Control Wonk* (blog), August 30, 2011, http://krepon.armscontrolwonk.com/archive/3211/de-alerting-and-de-legitimization.

12. Since the North Atlantic Treaty Organization (NATO) increased its conventional capabilities, witnessed by the Russians in the campaigns in Kosovo, the Russians became concerned that they "would no longer be able to defend [their] territory adequately from a limited war using conventional means." The result has been a steady increase of Russian reliance on tactical nuclear weapons and ballistic missiles. See Grant Schneider, "Tactical Nuclear Weapons, NATO and Russia" (paper presented at PONI Fall 2010 Conference, Aldermaston, UK, September 21, 2010), 50–51, http://csis.org/images/stories/poni/111007_Schneider.pdf.

13. Russell J. Leng, "Interstate Crisis Escalation and War," in *The Dynamics of Aggression*, eds. Michael Potegal and John F. Knutson (Hillsdale, NJ: Lawrence Erlbaum Associates, Inc., 1994), 308.

A nuclear "July Crisis"[14] would be devastating, especially with the knowledge it could have been avoided by prudent nuclear force posturing and the maintenance of a credible deterrent. When two powers have a significant and survivable portion of their nuclear arsenals on alert, the temptation to increase alert status in the event of a high-tension crisis is lower.

Russia is not the only nuclear power with which the United States has an unstable relationship, making preventing crisis escalation an even more important and relevant concern. Keir Lieber and Daryl Press argue that a weaker adversary's "fear of not surviving the conflict makes nuclear escalation as a means of forestalling defeat more likely."[15] Maintaining alert rates may prevent weaker adversaries, who view nuclear weapons as a balancing force against U.S. conventional superiority, from using nuclear weapons to stalemate a conventional war. The United States made this decision at Hiroshima and Nagasaki in 1945. In an escalation with an adversary, the president would likely re-alert de-alerted U.S. nuclear forces, an escalatory measure not necessary under the current posture. There is no way to reliably verify the alert status of a state's nuclear forces; states in an escalating crisis situation would most likely act upon worst-case assessments. The United States would not be free of the need to rapidly re-alert in a crisis, and a nuclear adversary in a tense situation would not be comforted by U.S. promises of a de-alerted status.

The knowledge that U.S. nuclear retaliation could occur within hours or days is an important part of deterrence. It serves as a backdrop that gives the United States strategic flexibility in responding to unexpected events in which no strategic warning allowed for the re-alerting of nuclear forces. The availability of these systems to the U.S. president as a retaliatory option does not mean a decision will be made to use them. In fact, nuclear weapons' purpose is to prevent the need for their use. As states increasingly view nuclear weapons as a valuable option for counteracting the superiority of U.S. conventional strength, the availability of nuclear weapons on alert becomes all the more valuable.

Improving the Nuclear Security Environment

The 2010 *Nuclear Posture Review Report* outlines what needs to be done to adapt to the new nuclear environment and identifies the risks associated with it, such as nuclear terrorism and proliferation. As part of that assessment the review examined the alert rates of U.S. nuclear forces and their utility, concluding that "this posture should be maintained."[16] It makes clear the importance of continued deterrence and speaks to the need for further improving the U.S. relationship with Russia to "create the conditions for moving toward a world without nuclear weapons."[17] The study showed that elements of international rela-

14. The "July Crisis" was a diplomatic crisis in July 1914 that resulted in the outbreak of World War I. Following the assassination of Archduke Franz Ferdinand, political tensions in the Balkans reached their breaking point, and the rapid mobilization of European armies began. Over the course of less than two weeks, the whole of Europe was dragged into war.

15. Lieber and Press, *Coercive Nuclear Campaigns in the 21st Century*, 36.

16. Department of Defense, *Nuclear Posture Review Report* (Washington, DC: Department of Defense, April 2010), 25, http://www.defense.gov/npr/docs/2010%20nuclear%20posture%20review%20report.pdf.

17. Ibid., 7.

tions need to change before alert rates and deterrence can or should change. Because de-alerting would be more destabilizing than not, changes in the international security environment should be pursued before another review of the alert status is conducted.

Concern about the reliability of Russia's early warning system provides a good example. To maintain the credibility and security of a deterrent, the system must be secure and effective. In the absence of a solution, serious crises are likely to occur. One such situation was the 1995 Norwegian rocket incident. The United States and Norway launched a rocket carrying scientific equipment to study the aurora borealis. The Russians mistook the rocket for a U.S. Trident SLBM, prompting Moscow to put its nuclear forces on high alert. The situation was resolved without resulting in a major crisis. However, it made evident the need for improved communication and more effective warning systems. Improving the early warning system would not only lower the chances of misunderstandings such as this, but also allow Russia to "consult to resolve concerns or ambiguities" and open up opportunities for more conversation between the two nations.[18] Proponents of de-alert see Russia's weak early warning system as an example that proves the risk of accidental launch; however de-alerting weapons does not eliminate the source of that risk. Improving the early warning system solves the overarching problem without destabilizing or devaluing the deterrent through de-alert.

Just as the Russian early warning system needs to be improved and modernized, so do U.S. nuclear forces. Former U.S. Air Force Chief of Staff and Strategic Air Command Commander General Larry Welch said, "It is time to drop such errant proposals as de-alerting and get on with the important job of preserving and updating a deterrent that, as the Constitution requires, so successfully 'provides for the common defense.'"[19] For this deterrent to continue to be successful, it needs to remain credible. Testing of new U.S. nuclear weapons designs is politically infeasible. For this reason, life-extension programs of the existing arsenal must be funded and fully implemented. Just as keeping these weapons on alert helps to maintain stability day-to-day and in crisis, their effectiveness keeps our nuclear relationships stable as well.

Conclusion

The United States should continue to pursue changes in the international security environment that would eventually reduce or eliminate the need for nuclear forces to remain on day-to-day alert. The existence of nuclear weapons inherently requires deterrence. To maintain a safe and credible deterrent for ourselves as well as our allies, as stipulated in the 2010 *Nuclear Posture Review Report*, alert levels must remain as they are until stabilizing changes can be achieved. Though not a perfect situation, the status quo is the best way to keep opportunists from taking a chance, misunderstandings from leading to escalation, and crises from becoming wars.

18. Woolf, "Nuclear Force Posture and Alert Rates," 5.

19. Peter Huessey, "Should the US De-alert its Nuclear Missiles?" Gatestone Institute, August 10, 2012, http://www.gatestoneinstitute.org/3266/us-nuclear-missiles-alert.